D0571076

Eric Zweig

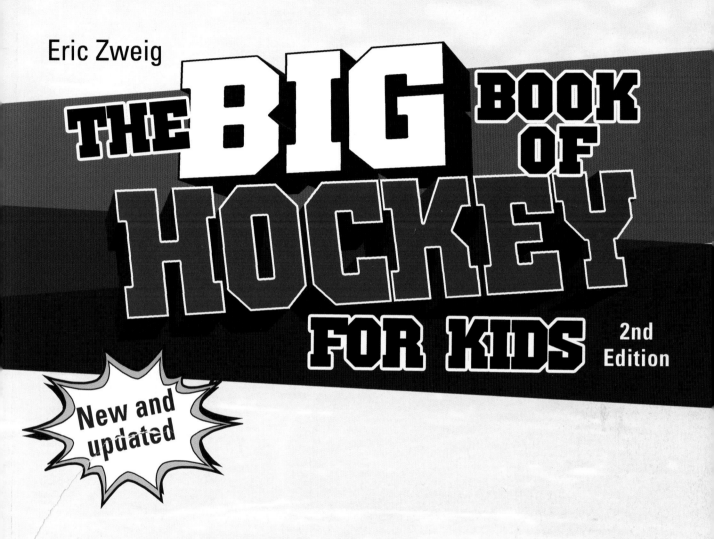

THE BIG BOOK OF HOCKEY FOR KIDS

2nd Edition

New and updated

Eric Zweig

Scholastic Canada Ltd.

Toronto New York London Auckland Sydney
Mexico City New Delhi Hong Kong Buenos Aires

Scholastic Canada Ltd.
604 King Street West, Toronto, Ontario M5V 1E1, Canada

Scholastic Inc.
557 Broadway, New York, NY 10012, USA

Scholastic Australia Pty Limited
PO Box 579, Gosford, NSW 2250, Australia

Scholastic New Zealand Limited
Private Bag 94407, Botany, Manukau 2163, New Zealand

Scholastic Children's Books
Euston House, 24 Eversholt Street, London NW1 1DB, UK

www.scholastic.ca

For my family and friends who made sports so much fun when I was growing up.
—E.Z.

Credits: see page 134

Library and Archives Canada Cataloguing in Publication

Zweig, Eric, 1963-, author
The big book of hockey for kids / Eric Zweig. -- Second edition.

ISBN 978-1-4431-4867-2 (hardcover)

1. Hockey--Miscellanea--Juvenile literature. 2. National Hockey
League--Miscellanea--Juvenile literature. I. Title.

GV847.25.Z938 2017   j796.962   C2017-902185-0

5 4 3 2 1   Printed in Malaysia 108   17 18 19 20 21

TABLE OF CONTENTS

IN THE BEGINNING

WHO STARTED THIS GAME, ANYWAY?

There's no easy answer to the question, "Who invented hockey?" In fact, there's probably no answer at all. Hockey didn't just appear one day, with a set of rules and players who knew exactly what to do. It evolved over the centuries from many different types of ball-and-stick games. These games weren't always played on ice, but they all played a part in helping to form the game Canadians love.

A LONG TIME AGO IN A DESERT FAR, FAR AWAY . . .

Iraq was once part of an area known as Mesopotamia. That area is referred to as "the cradle of civilization." Was it also the cradle of hockey? Not the hockey we've come to know and love, but clearly something similar. Archaeologists have found what is probably the earliest reference to a hockey-like game. Twelve clay tablets dating back almost 5,000 years to about 2700 B.C.E. tell the story of a king named Gilgamesh who was a warrior and an athlete. The twelfth tablet tells of a game he played called *Pukku–Mikku*, which was played on a flat, dirt surface using a curved stick and a circular wooden ring. *Mikku* refers to the stick, while the word *Pukku* — which even looks and sounds a bit like the word puck — was the wooden ring.

Similar games would be played in other ancient civilizations over the centuries. In Egypt, a painting from around 2050 B.C.E. was found in a tomb. In it, two men are carrying wooden sticks and there is a small ball on the ground between them. It looks like the men are lined up for a faceoff. And the Greeks seemed to have their own game: historians have found marble carvings from 500 B.C.E. that show a similar game. Seems like even the ancients knew how much fun hockey could be!

OTHER EARLY GAMES

Hurling is an Irish game that is older than Ireland itself. It dates back to at least 1272 B.C.E. Early versions of the game could involve hundreds of players and last for days. Hurling was so rough that it was banned during the 1300s because of the violence (sound familiar?), but the game stuck around and was more popular than ever during the 1700s. New rules were written down during the 1800s to make the game more modern.

Hurling is still popular in Ireland today, though they've cut back on the number of players. It's played on a large field where players use a wooden stick known as a hurley (the sport itself is often called hurley in North America) and a small leather ball that looks like a baseball. There are 15 players on each team. They can hit the ball in the air or on the ground and can also use their feet or hands to make a pass. The object of the game is to hit the ball between the other team's goal posts, either over the crossbar for one point or into the net under the crossbar for three points.

Shinty is a Scottish game that is very similar to hurling and has a similar history. Shinty is a little bit more like field hockey than hurling is, but like hurling, the ball can be hit out of the air and

In the January 31, 1835, edition of Britain's *The Penny Magazine*, a writer described watching a game of shinty in which "one of the players, having gained possession of the ball, contrived to run a mile with it in his hand, pursued by both his own and the adverse party . . ."

players can use both sides of their sticks. Traditionally, shinty was played in the winter. Whole villages would gather on New Year's Day for games that involved hundreds of players. Today, shinty is played with 12 players on each team.

Bandy is a game played on a large ice surface with players using skates, stick and a ball. It looks somewhat like field hockey on ice, and shares many rules in common with soccer. Bandy was played in Russia in the early 1700s, and may date as far back as the 10th century. It became popular in England during the 1800s and spread to countries such as Norway, Finland and Sweden around the end of that century. In the early 1900s, bandy was much more popular than hockey was in Europe. Though the game is not as well known today, bandy is still played in all those countries and a few others too.

INDIGENOUS HOCKEY

Indigenous people in North America already had their own forms of ball-and-stick games, and when people from England, Ireland and Scotland began to settle in Canada in the 1700s and 1800s, they brought games like hurly, shinty and bandy with them, too. Some Indigenous people already played games on ice, and when the weather got cold in winter, the newcomers to Canada began to play their games on frozen lakes and rivers.

PUTTING THE GAME ON ICE

Windsor, Nova Scotia, claims to be the birthplace of hockey. Windsor, so the story goes, is where the game of hurley was first played on ice, on the frozen water of Long Pond. It was first played around 1800 by students at King's College.

Windsor's claim is based on the writings of a man named Thomas Chandler Haliburton. Haliburton was born in Windsor in 1796 and graduated from King's College in 1815. In a book called *The Attaché* he wrote in 1844, Haliburton had his hero, Sam Slick, recall his younger days at King's College. Slick remembered the boys, "yelpin', hollerin', and whoopin' like mad with pleasure," as they played "hurley on the Long Pond ice."

There's lots of evidence to prove that games like hurley were played on the ice all around Nova Scotia in the early 1800s, but it may not have been the first place it was played. Swedish researchers Carl Giden and Patrick Houda are always hunting for stories about early forms of hockey. They've found stories about hurley being played on the ice in New York and Philadelphia as early as the 1780s! There's also a picture that was drawn in London, England, in 1797, showing a boy skating on a river with a stick in his hand and something that looks an awful lot like a puck on the ice in front of him.

IN THE CREASE

There's another story about how hockey got its name. According to some, a British military man named Colonel Hockey was stationed at Fort Edward in Windsor, Nova Scotia, in the early 1800s. Some say he created the game to keep his troops in shape, but there is no documented proof of this.

In December 1796, it was cold enough in London, England, for the Thames River to freeze over. The "puck" the boy is using is most likely a bung — a plug for a barrel — made out of wood or cork.

HOW HOCKEY GOT ITS NAME

Hok or *Hak* is an old word from Germanic languages that means "hook." In French, there is a similar word, *hoquet*, that means "curved stick" but was usually used to refer to a shepherd's crook. The word "hockey" more than likely comes from these old words.

The earliest use of the word "hockey" seems to appear in a book of games for children called *Juvenile Sports and Pastimes*. It was first published in London, England, in 1773. In the book, author Richard Johnson says that he played hockey as a boy in school in the 1740s. He writes about how much fun the game is to play, and gives his young readers instructions on how to play it. However, in his description, and in the drawings that appear in the book, it's clear the game he's talking about was played on a field, and not on the ice. Still, the word hockey (or sometimes hawkey) had become pretty common in England by the 1830s — although it usually meant "a curved or bent stick" rather than a game that was played with a curved stick.

THE EVOLUTION OF HOCKEY

The theory of evolution was first put forward by Charles Darwin to explain the history of life on earth. He wrote about it in a book called *On the Origin of Species* that was published in 1859. What does this have to do with hockey? Nothing, really. Still, Charles Darwin offers some pretty good proof that a game called hockey was being played on the ice in England by the early 1800s — even if he wasn't so sure of the spelling!

In 2014, Carl Giden and Patrick Houda published a book with Canadian hockey researcher Jean-Patrice Martel. They called their book *On the Origin of Hockey*. The similarity to Darwin's title was no coincidence! Among the many fascinating stories they present about the early history of hockey is a letter Charles Darwin wrote to his son William on March 1, 1853, when William was attending Shrewsbury School. In it, Darwin asks: "Have you got a pretty good pond to skate on? I used to be very fond of playing at Hocky on the ice in skates." Since Darwin himself had been a student at

Shrewsbury from 1818 to 1825, that's pretty good proof that not just field hockey but ice hockey has been played in England for a very long time.

COMING INDOORS

There are plenty of stories from different parts of Canada, the United States and England that show how popular outdoor hockey had become between 1825 and 1869. It wasn't until a few years later that the game officially moved indoors and started to become the game we play today.

Sometime around 1873, a group of young men in Montreal began playing games of hockey at the city's Victoria Skating Rink. On March 3, 1875, they gave the first public demonstration. There were nine men on the ice for each team.

The men usually played hockey with a rubber ball, but on this night they used a flat piece of wood so that it wouldn't bounce around so much and fly into the crowd of spectators.

Soon other groups in Montreal began taking up the game. On February 1, 1877, McGill University in Montreal created the first official hockey team. On February 27, 1877, the *Montreal Gazette* printed the first set of hockey rules. Those rules were very similar to ones used to play field hockey in England but they would help to make ice hockey very popular in Canada. Whether it was being played indoors or out, hockey was being played all across the country by the 1890s. Soon, there would be the Stanley Cup to give all the top leagues across Canada a national championship trophy to shoot for.

A colourized postcard image of the Victoria Skating Rink, taken in the 1890s. The size of the ice helped set the standard for hockey rinks, and the first-ever Stanley Cup playoff game was held there March 17, 1894.

LEAGUE HISTORY

THE FIRST LEAGUE

If the NHL had a family tree, its great-great-great grandparent would be the Amateur Hockey Association of Canada (AHAC). This league was formed in Montreal on December 8, 1886. There were five teams during the 1886–87 season: four of them from Montreal, the fifth from Ottawa. Though the word Canada was right there in its name, the league only ever had teams in Montreal, Ottawa and Quebec City.

THE NHL FAMILY TREE

Though there would soon be leagues and teams playing hockey all across the country, the fact that most of the country's population lived in Quebec and Ontario meant the leagues in those provinces were usually considered the most important ones. The leagues shown below were all based in Ontario and Quebec.

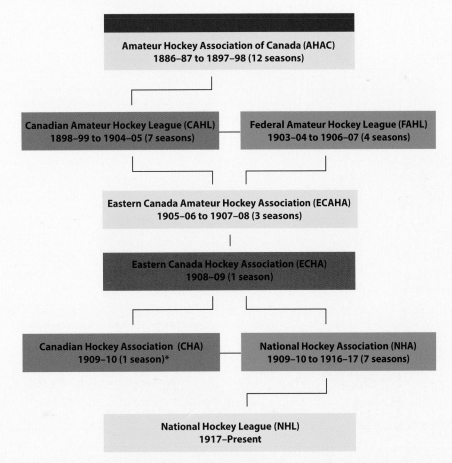

Amateur Hockey Association of Canada (AHAC)
1886–87 to 1897–98 (12 seasons)

Canadian Amateur Hockey League (CAHL)
1898–99 to 1904–05 (7 seasons)

Federal Amateur Hockey League (FAHL)
1903–04 to 1906–07 (4 seasons)

Eastern Canada Amateur Hockey Association (ECAHA)
1905–06 to 1907–08 (3 seasons)

Eastern Canada Hockey Association (ECHA)
1908–09 (1 season)

Canadian Hockey Association (CHA)
1909–10 (1 season)*

National Hockey Association (NHA)
1909–10 to 1916–17 (7 seasons)

National Hockey League (NHL)
1917–Present

*The Canadian Hockey Association only lasted a few games. Some of its teams then joined the National Hockey Association.

GOING PRO

As the names of most of the early leagues show, hockey was an amateur game for many years. That meant none of the players got paid. In fact all sports in Canada were amateur sports. Most people in the country believed that athletes shouldn't be paid to play games; sports should be played only for enjoyment. But as hockey and other sports became more popular, teams realized they had to start paying their players if they wanted to get the top talent.

Baseball teams in the United States had started paying players as early as 1869. The first pro hockey leagues began in the United States in the early 1900s.

The first Canadian league to go pro was the Eastern Canada Amateur Hockey Association (ECAHA). In November 1906, the league agreed to let amateurs and pros play together. Some teams decided to pay their players, but others didn't. The Montreal Wanderers were one of the teams in the ECAHA that started paying players. Since the Wanderers were the Stanley Cup champions, the trustees in charge of the Cup had to agree to let it become a professional trophy. Many people disagreed, but they did it anyway. Ever since, only professional teams have played for the Stanley Cup. By 1908, some of the leagues in Canada's western provinces and in the Maritimes had become pro as well, but many others remained amateur. So a new trophy called the Allan Cup was donated to recognize the country's amateur champions. The Allan Cup still exists, and amateur teams still play for it every year, but the trophy gets nowhere near the attention that the Stanley Cup does.

THE NATIONAL HOCKEY ASSOCIATION

The NHA was organized at a meeting in Montreal on December 2, 1909. It was formed by the Montreal Wanderers and a team from the small town of Renfrew, Ontario. They were angry because they had been left out when the Eastern Canada Hockey Association reorganized itself as the Canadian Hockey Association (CHA). The two new leagues went to battle trying to sign the best players. The NHA was willing to pay higher salaries, so more players wanted to sign with their teams. When two of the teams in the CHA agreed to leave their league to join the NHA, the CHA went out of business and the NHA emerged as the top league in hockey.

A Montreal Wanderers sweater belonging to Cecil Blachford, who was on the team when they won Stanley Cup Championships in 1906, 1907, 1908 and 1910.

THE NHL IS BORN

World War I took its toll on all aspects of life in Canada. With men away fighting, women working in factories, and so many deaths and horrible injuries, the years from 1914 to 1918 were difficult ones.

Many people wondered if it was right for any strong, healthy man to play hockey or any other sport when there was a war on. Many players chose to give up the game to join the army or take other jobs that helped the war effort. During the 1916–17 season, the NHA even had a team of hockey-playing soldiers called the 228th Battalion, but the team was called to serve overseas before the season was over. Fans were starting to lose interest in hockey, and the sport was clearly in trouble.

In November 1917 the NHA closed down. But it didn't really go away. Most of the owners of the NHA teams voted to form a brand new organization. They called it

OTHER EARLY LEAGUES

Here is a list of other early hockey leagues in Canada that once competed for the Stanley Cup. Years marked in bold mean a Stanley Cup victory.

- Ontario Hockey Association
  1895, 1899, 1902, 1904
- Manitoba and Northwest Hockey Association
  1896, 1899, 1900, **1901**, **1902**, 1903, 1904
- Central Canada Hockey Association (based in Ontario)
  1897
- Halifax/Nova Scotia/Maritime Hockey League
  1900, 1906
- Western Canada Hockey Association (based in Manitoba)
  1904
- Manitoba Hockey League (amateur)
  1905
- Canadian Intercollegiate Hockey Union (based in Ontario and Quebec)
  1906

- Manitoba Hockey League (professional)
  1907, 1908
- Ontario Professional Hockey League
  1908, 1910, 1911
- Interprovincial Hockey League (based in Saskatchewan and Alberta)
  1908
- Alberta Professional Hockey League
  1910
- New Ontario Hockey League (based in Northern Ontario)
  1911
- Maritime Professional Hockey League (based in New Brunswick and Nova Scotia)
  1912, 1913

the National Hockey *League*. Many sources say the NHL began on November 22, 1917, but newspaper stories written at the time show that the league was actually formed four days later, on November 26, 1917.

There is no doubt that the effects of World War I had hurt the NHA, but another reason the NHL was formed was to get rid of an unpopular team owner. Eddie Livingstone owned the Toronto Blueshirts, and the rest of the NHA owners didn't like him. At first the NHL wasn't even going to include Toronto in the new league. It was to be made up of the Ottawa Senators, the Montreal Canadiens, the Montreal Wanderers and the Quebec Bulldogs. It was only because the owners in Quebec decided that they couldn't get enough good players that the decision was made to add a team in Toronto. Even though Toronto would have almost the exact same lineup as Livingstone's Blueshirts, the team was

awarded to the men who owned the Toronto arena where the team played. For that reason, Toronto's first NHL team became known as the Toronto Arenas.

The Arenas were named after their home ice, Arena Gardens. When it opened in 1912, it was the biggest indoor rink in the world, with seating for 7500 and artificial ice-making capabilities.

WESTERN RIVALS

Though it was the NHA that would later become the NHL, there was another professional league in this era that did a great deal to modernize the game of hockey: the Pacific Coast Hockey Association (PCHA).

In 1911, Lester Patrick and his younger brother Frank created the PCHA, which lasted until the 1923–1924 season. They had grown up in Montreal and were

The Toronto Blueshirts won the city's first Stanley Cup. They were the 1914 NHA champions.

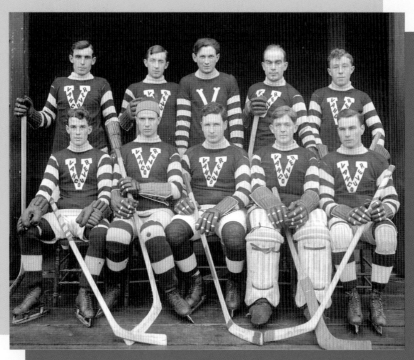

In 1915 the Vancouver Millionaires swept the Ottawa Senators in three straight games to win the Stanley Cup, outscoring them 26–8 in the series.

star players in the East before their family moved west to British Columbia. Because of the warmer climate on the West Coast, the Patrick family built the first artificial ice rinks in Canada in Vancouver and Victoria. Frank owned the PCHA team in Vancouver, which he called the Millionaires. He was also the coach, general manager and a star player with the team. Lester had all the same duties with the PCHA team in Victoria, which became known as the Aristocrats. Some rules and innovations they helped give to modern hockey include:

- removing the rule that goalies had to play standing up
- adding numbers to players' sweaters
- adding the first blue lines to the ice
- allowing forward passing
- creating the penalty shot
- creating the playoffs

MOVING ON

Before the 1924–25 season, the Patrick brothers' teams in Vancouver and Victoria joined up with the Calgary Tigers, Edmonton Eskimos, Regina Capitals and Saskatoon Sheiks as part of the Western Canada Hockey League (WCHL). A year later, the Capitals moved to Portland, Oregon, and the word "Canada" was dropped from the league name. The Western Hockey League only lasted for the 1925–26 season. When the league folded, many of its players found their way onto the rosters of NHL teams, and the NHL became the undisputed top league in all of hockey.

LORD STANLEY AND HIS CUP

A BIG BOOST FOR HOCKEY

In 1883, the city of Montreal hosted a Winter Carnival that attracted people from around the world. One of the biggest events was the world's first hockey tournament. Three teams from Montreal and one from Quebec City took part, but the popularity of the entire carnival gave a big boost to the new sport.

The Montreal Winter Carnival and its hockey tournament were held again in 1884, 1885, 1887 and 1889. Canada's new governor general — Lord Stanley of Preston — travelled from Ottawa to watch his first hockey game at the carnival in 1889. A few years later, Lord Stanley would give hockey an even bigger boost.

HOCKEY'S ROYAL FAMILY

Frederick Arthur Stanley arrived in Canada on June 9, 1888, to begin his term as Governor General. Lord Stanley's father was a former prime minister of England, and Lord Stanley himself had served as a politician for many years.

Like a great many British aristocrats of his day, Lord Stanley was an active sportsman. He and his family became big fans of the new sports they found in Canada. Snowshoeing and toboggan parties became a regular part of the winter activities at Rideau Hall, the Governor General's home. Soon hockey became a favourite pastime as well.

Lord Stanley and his wife had seven sons and a daughter, and all of the children became hockey players. An outdoor rink was set up at Rideau Hall, and sons Edward, Arthur and Algernon became members of a team known as the Rideau Rebels. James Creighton (see page 37-38), who had moved from Montreal to Ottawa around 1882, also played for the Rebels. The team would travel across Ontario in Lord Stanley's private rail car to play games. Daughter Isobel Stanley became a hockey player, too, and a picture of her taken around 1890 playing with other ladies on the ice at Rideau Hall is believed to be the earliest image of women's hockey.

Lord Frederick Arthur Stanley, of Preston, England, who gave hockey the coveted Stanley Cup.

STANLEY CUP HISTORY LESSON

Who wouldn't want to name an NHL trophy after himself? Lord Stanley, that's who. When he first commissioned the prize, he called it the Dominion Hockey Challenge Cup and had the name engraved on the bowl. However, the two trustees who he put in charge of the new trophy decided to call it the Stanley Cup in his honour.

Lord Stanley chose the name Dominion because Canada was known back then as the Dominion of Canada.

When the Cup was first presented in 1893, there were many leagues all across the country. At the time, cold weather was the only way to make ice and trains were the only way to travel, so schedules had to be short and teams had to be pretty close to each other. To make sure that teams from different parts of the country had a

THE STANLEY CUP IS BORN

On March 18, 1892, a banquet was held in Ottawa honouring the Ottawa Hockey Club. The team had enjoyed a very good season and, though they hadn't won their league championship, most hockey fans still believed that Ottawa was the best team that winter. Many of them were unhappy with the way the championship had been decided.

Lord Stanley was not at the banquet that night, but a letter he had written was read to the crowd:

The original Stanley Cup was actually named the Dominion Hockey Challenge Cup. It's on display at the Hockey Hall of Fame in Toronto, Ontario.

the east and the PCHA in the west were the two top leagues in hockey. That year, the trustees agreed to change the format to a best-of-five series between the two league champions. In this way, the Stanley Cup Final became like the World Series in baseball. In fact, it was usually referred to as "The World's Hockey Series" or "The World Series of Hockey." Since it could take almost a whole week to travel across the country by train, all the games were played in an eastern city one year and a western city the next. When the NHL took over from the NHA for the 1917–18 season, they continued this Stanley Cup relationship with the PCHA. The east-west format lasted through the 1925–26 season.

When professional hockey collapsed in the west, the NHL was left as the top league in all of hockey. Since the 1926–27 season, only teams from the NHL have been allowed to compete for the Stanley Cup.

chance to win the Stanley Cup, it had to be a challenge trophy. That meant that the champions from the different leagues across the country got to challenge the current Stanley Cup champion to a special playoff series. Usually these challenge series were played at the end of the season, but sometimes they were played before the new season started. Sometimes, they were even played right in the middle of the schedule! This challenge format lasted from 1893 to 1913.

By the winter of 1913–14, the NHA in

Canadian brothers Frank and Lester Patrick formed the Seattle Metropolitans in 1915. Lester Patrick as a player, coach and manager won six Stanley Cups.

first American team to play for the Cup. They lost to the Montreal Canadiens. In 1917, the Seattle Metropolitans beat the Canadiens to become the first American team to win the Cup.

CANCELLED CUP

In 1919, the Montreal Canadiens faced the Seattle Metropolitans in a Stanley Cup rematch. Fans expected an exciting series, but what they got was a tragedy. The last game of the Stanley Cup Final had to be cancelled when several players became sick with the deadly Spanish Flu. This disease, which killed millions of people around the world, took the life of Canadiens star Joe Hall a few days after the series was cancelled.

BEST OF SEVEN

These days in the NHL, it takes four rounds of playoffs to win the Stanley Cup, and in each series a team has to be the first to win four out of a possible seven games. For much of the NHL's early history, a team could win the Stanley Cup in as few as two playoff rounds, and for some years, they'd only have to win two out of three games in the Finals. The first best-of-seven series in the Stanley Cup Final was played in 1939 when Boston beat Toronto four games to one. Two years later, in 1941, the Bruins became the first team to sweep to the Stanley Cup when they beat the Detroit Red Wings in four straight games. The first time that the Stanley Cup Final went to seven games was in 1942. That year, Detroit jumped

Legendary player and coach Clarence "Hap" Day holds the Stanley Cup after the Leafs' 1942 victory. The Cup is one of the few trophies that have entire teams' names engraved on them.

SOUTH OF THE BORDER

When the Stanley Cup was donated in 1893, it was to reward the championship team in Canada. Over the years, the trustees turned down challenges from any American teams. They wouldn't even let two Canadian teams play for the Cup in any American city. The PCHA began adding teams in the United States for the 1914–15 season. A year later, the trustees decided to allow American teams to play for the Stanley Cup. In 1916, the Portland Rosebuds from Portland, Oregon (Portland is known as "The Rose City"), were the

NHL STANLEY CUP DYNASTIES

Ottawa Senators — *1920, 1921, 1923, 1927*

Toronto Maple Leafs — *1947, 1948, 1949, 1951*

Detroit Red Wings — *1950 , 1952, 1954, 1955*

Montreal Canadiens — *1956, 1957, 1958, 1959, 1960*

Toronto Maple Leafs — *1962, 1963, 1964, 1967*

Montreal Canadiens — *1965, 1966, 1968, 1969*

Montreal Canadiens — *1976, 1977, 1978, 1979*

New York Islanders — *1980 , 1981, 1982, 1983*

Edmonton Oilers — *1984, 1985, 1987, 1988, 1990*

ahead of Toronto with three straight wins, but the Maple Leafs rallied to win the next four in a row. A few other teams in NHL history have come back to win a series after losing the first three games, but no one else has ever done it in the Stanley Cup Final.

THE AGE OF THE DYNASTIES

These days, it's tough to keep a team together for very long. With salary caps and giant contracts, free agents move around a lot. That makes it hard to win championships in back-to-back seasons, let alone three years or more in a row. Winning the Stanley Cup three straight times or more is what gets a team labelled a dynasty. The term is also applied to teams that win four or five championships in a space of six or seven years.

STANLEY CUP ADVENTURES

In 1993, the NHL marked the Stanley Cup's 100th birthday. They thought that letting each player on the winning team spend a whole a day with the Cup would be a great way to celebrate. It turned out to be very popular with players and with fans too. So, ever since 1995, the NHL has given all the players and the staff on the winning team their own special day to spend with the Stanley Cup that summer.

A player's day with the Stanley Cup often involves taking it to his hometown,

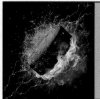

Freaky Fact
Bill Barilko scored the Stanley Cup winner in 1951 for the Maple Leafs but was killed in a plane crash in the northern Ontario wilderness that summer. The Maple Leafs didn't win the Cup again until 1962. A few weeks later, the wreckage of Barilko's plane was finally found.

which these days, might be in a lot of different countries around the world. The Stanley Cup has been to beaches, mountaintops and igloos. It's been to hospitals to cheer up patients and to parties just to have fun. Lots of players have eaten lots of different foods — like ice cream, popcorn or perogies — right out of the Stanley Cup bowl.

Wherever the Stanley Cup goes, someone from the Hockey Hall of Fame is there with it to make sure it doesn't get into too much trouble. Still, it's been known to get stuck in traffic, miss its airplane, or fall off a table and need some repairs. But these sorts of problems are nothing like the strange situations the Stanley Cup found itself in the early days of hockey history.

One of the strangest stories in Stanley Cup history is a tale told from 1905 when a few winning members of the Ottawa Silver Seven were said to have tried to kick the original Stanley Cup bowl across the city's Rideau Canal. It's one of the most famous legends in Stanley Cup history … but it probably didn't really happen! But it is true that in 1924, a carload of Montreal Canadiens players left the Stanley Cup by the side of the road when they had to change a flat tire. It wasn't until the players arrived at a team party that they realized what happened. So they got back in the car, and once again drove through the streets of Montreal. Lucky for them, they found the Cup right where they left it, still sitting on the curb!

Dustin Byfuglien takes the cup ATVing after the Chicago Blackhawks 2010 championship win. Between adventures, the cup travels in a special padded case to keep it safe.

TEAM SPIRIT

FIRST NHL TEAMS

When the NHL began playing its first season on December 19, 1917, there were only four teams in the league. The first two games that night featured the Ottawa Senators hosting the Montreal Canadiens and the Toronto Arenas visiting the Montreal Wanderers. The Canadiens beat the Senators 7–4 and the Wanderers beat the Arenas 10–9. It was the only NHL game the Wanderers ever won. They lost their next three in a row, and then withdrew from the league after a fire destroyed the Montreal Arena on January 2, 1918.

Montreal Canadiens goalie Carey Price stops a shot by Toronto Maple Leafs rookie Auston Matthews in the third period of a game on January 7, 2017. The Canadiens won 5–3.

MONTREAL CANADIENS

Franchise Formed: 1909
First NHL Season: 1917–18
Star Players: Jean Beliveau, Toe Blake, Yvan Cournoyer, Ken Dryden, Bill Durnan, Bob Gainey, Alex Galchenyuk, Bernie Geoffrion, George Hainsworth, Doug Harvey, Aurel Joliat, Elmer Lach, Guy Lafleur, Newsy Lalonde, Jacques Lemaire, Frank Mahovlich, Peter Mahovlich, Joe Malone, Dickie Moore, Howie Morenz, Max Pacioretty, Jacques Plante, Carey Price, Henri Richard, Maurice Richard, Larry Robinson, Patrick Roy, Serge Savard, Georges Vezina

HISTORIC MOMENTS

- Hold record for most Stanley Cup wins in hockey history (24)

- Have won more games and scored more goals than any team in NHL history

- Hold record for most points in one NHL season (132: 60 wins, 8 losses, 12 ties in 1976–77)

TORONTO MAPLE LEAFS (Previously Arenas and St. Patricks)

Franchise Formed: 1912 (as Toronto Blueshirts)
First NHL Season: 1917–18
First Season as St. Patricks: 1919–20
First Season as Maple Leafs: 1926–27

Star Players: Syl Apps, George Armstrong, Ace Bailey, Johnny Bower, Turk Broda, King Clancy, Wendel Clark, Charlie Conacher, Hap Day, Babe Dye, Doug Gilmour, Paul Henderson, Tim Horton, Busher Jackson, Red Kelly, Ted Kennedy, Dave Keon, Frank Mahovlich, Auston Matthews, Lanny McDonald, Joe Primeau, Borje Salming, Darryl Sittler, Mats Sundin, Rick Vaive

HISTORIC MOMENTS

- Won first NHL Championship in 1917–18

- Name changed to Maple Leafs by new owner Conn Smythe on February 14, 1927

- First NHL team to win the Stanley Cup in three straight seasons (1946–47, 1947–48, 1948–49)

TEAMS COME AND GO

The NHL began to grow during the 1920s. The first "new" team to join the league wasn't really a new team at all. Quebec City was supposed to be part of the NHL when it was formed in 1917, but the team didn't actually play until the 1919–20 season. Quebec had always been known as the Bulldogs in the NHA, but some newspapers called their NHL team the Athletics.

Quebec lasted only one season in the NHL. The Hamilton Tigers replaced them in 1920–21. Then the Montreal Maroons and the Boston Bruins joined, followed by the New York Americans, who replaced the Tigers in 1925–26. The NHL also added another new team called the Pittsburgh Pirates that year. A year later, the New York Rangers came on board, along with new teams in Detroit and Chicago.

The NHL now had 10 teams playing in two divisions, but then the Great Depression came, affecting all aspects of life. Many people lost their jobs and many companies went out of business. Hockey teams had trouble, too. Both Ottawa and Pittsburgh moved to new cities to try to stay alive, but soon both franchises had to drop out. Later, the Maroons and Americans folded, too.

BOSTON BRUINS

First NHL Season: 1924–25
Star Players: Patrice Bergeron, Raymond Bourque, Frank Brimsek, Johnny Bucyk, Wayne Cashman, Zdeno Chara, Gerry Cheevers, Dit Clapper, Bill Cowley, Phil Esposito, Lionel Hitchman, Brad Marchand, Rick Middleton, Cam Neely, Terry O'Reilly, Bobby Orr, Brad Park, Tuukka Rask, Jean Ratelle, Milt Schmidt, Eddie Shore, Tiny Thompson, Cooney Weiland

The New York Rangers' Mark Messier (left) and Eric Lindros celebrate a goal against the Boston Bruins in the first period at Madison Square Garden in their December 8, 2002, game. The Bruins came back to win it 4–1.

HISTORIC MOMENTS

- First NHL team in an American city

- Winning percentage of .875 (38–5–1) in 1929–30 remains an NHL record

- Only team in history to have players finish 1–2–3–4 in the NHL scoring race . . . and they did it twice (Phil Esposito, Bobby Orr, Johnny Bucyk, Ken Hodge in 1970–71; Esposito, Orr, Hodge, Wayne Cashman in 1973–74)

THE ORIGINAL SIX

By the 1942–43 season, the NHL was left with only six teams: the Montreal Canadiens, Toronto Maple Leafs, Boston Bruins, New York Rangers, Detroit Red Wings and Chicago Blackhawks. Though only Montreal and Toronto were actually around when the league began, over the years these six teams have come to be known as the NHL's "Original Six."

These six teams were the only teams in the NHL for 25 years, from 1942–43 through 1966–67. During that time, the NHL schedule grew from 50 games to 70 and team rivalries became intense. Even today, there are many fans who get an extra feeling of excitement for games between two Original Six teams. With just six teams in the NHL, only the very best players got a chance to play. To this day, stars of the era such as Maurice Richard, Gordie Howe, Bobby Hull and Jean Beliveau are remembered with a special affection.

Toronto, Montreal and Detroit dominated the Original Six era. Together they won the Stanley Cup 24 times in those 25 years, with the Canadiens winning ten times, the Maple Leafs nine and Detroit five.

NEW YORK RANGERS

First NHL Season: 1926–27
Star Players: Andy Bathgate, Frank Boucher, Bill Cook, Bun Cook, Phil Esposito, Bill Gadsby, Ed Giacomin, Rod Gilbert, Adam Graves, Wayne Gretzky, Vic Hadfield, Bryan Hextall Sr., Harry Howell, Ching Johnson, Brian Leetch, Henrik Lundqvist, Mark Messier, Brad Park, Lynn Patrick, Jean Ratelle, Chuck Rayner, Mike Richter, Gump Worsley

HISTORIC MOMENTS

- Won the Stanley Cup in their second season (1927–28)

- After Cup wins in 1932–33 and 1939–40, went a record 54 years before winning again in 1993–94

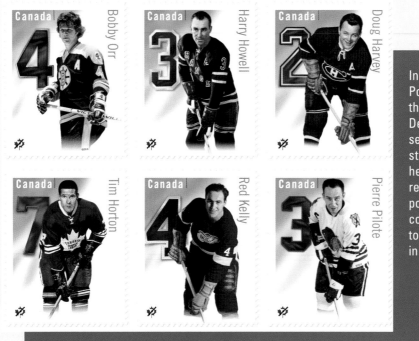

In 2014 Canada Post released the Original Six Defencemen series, featuring star players who helped define or revolutionize the position. Many consider this era to be a golden time in hockey's history.

CHICAGO BLACKHAWKS (Previously Black Hawks)

First NHL Season: 1926–27
Star Players: Tony Amonte, Ed Belfour, Doug Bentley, Max Bentley, Chris Chelios, Tony Esposito, Bill Gadsby, Charlie Gardiner, Glenn Hall, Marian Hossa, Bobby Hull, Dennis Hull, Dick Irvin, Patrick Kane, Duncan Keith, Steve Larmer, Stan Mikita, Bill Mosienko, Pierre Pilote, Jeremy Roenick, Denis Savard, Jonathan Toews, Doug Wilson, Ken Wharram

HISTORIC MOMENTS

- Team name was written as two words (Black Hawks) until 1985–86
- Ended a 49-year Stanley Cup drought in 2009–10 when Patrick Kane scored the winning goal in overtime

DETROIT RED WINGS (Previously Cougars and Falcons)

First NHL Season: 1926–27
First Season as Falcons: 1930–31
First Season as Red Wings: 1932–33
Star Players: Sid Abel, Larry Aurie, Pavel Datsyuk, Alex Delvecchio, Sergei Fedorov, Viacheslav Fetisov, Ebbie Goodfellow, Glenn Hall, Gordie Howe, Syd Howe, Red Kelly, Igor Larionov, Nicklas Lidstrom, Herbie Lewis, Ted Lindsay, Marcel Pronovost, Chris Osgood, Mickey Redmond,

Brendan Shanahan, Terry Sawchuk, Norm Ullman, Mike Vernon, Steve Yzerman, Henrik Zetterberg

HISTORIC MOMENTS

- Back-to-back Stanley Cups in 1935–36 and 1936–37, 1953–54 and 1954–55 and 1996–97 and 1997–98

- Finished in first place in the NHL standings for a record seven straight seasons (1948–49 to 1954–55)

- Hold record for most wins in one season (62 in 1995–96)

THE EXPANSION ERA BEGINS

With the end of World War II in 1945, there were good times ahead for Canada and the United States. The economy was booming and families were growing. Everything seemed to be getting bigger and better by the 1950s. Soon baseball and football began adding new teams, but the NHL stuck with its same six franchises.

Finally, on February 9, 1966, the NHL announced a plan to add six new teams: the Philadelphia Flyers, Pittsburgh Penguins, St. Louis Blues, Los Angeles Kings, Oakland Seals and Minnesota North Stars. On June 6, 1967, the NHL held its first Expansion Draft. Each new team picked 20 players and entered the NHL for the 1967–68 season. The Original Six teams were kept together in the East Division, while the six new teams played in the West. The playoff format guaranteed a new team would face an old team in the Stanley Cup Final for the next three years.

The NHL owners had always worried that there would not be enough talented players to grow beyond six teams. It did take a few years before the new NHL teams caught up with the best of the older ones, but it was soon clear that there was plenty of skill to go around. Expansion proved to be so popular that the NHL added six more teams during the 1970s, for a total of 18, before shrinking back to 17 in 1978.

PHILADELPHIA FLYERS

First NHL Season: 1967–68
Star Players: Bill Barber, Bobby Clarke, Claude Giroux, Ron Hextall, Mark Howe, Tim Kerr, Reggie Leach, John LeClair, Eric Lindros, Rick MacLeish, Bernie Parent, Brian Propp, Mark Recchi, Dave Schultz, Wayne Simmonds, Rick Tocchet

HISTORIC MOMENTS

- Became first modern expansion team to win the Stanley Cup (1973–1974)

- Earned the nickname "Broad Street Bullies" for their rough tactics in the 1970s

PITTSBURGH PENGUINS

First NHL Season: 1967–68

Star Players: Syl Apps Jr., Tom Barrasso, Paul Coffey, Sidney Crosby, John Cullen, Marc-Andre Fleury, Ron Francis, Jaromir Jagr, Rick Kehoe, Phil Kessel, Pierre Larouche, Mario Lemieux, Kris Letang, Evgeni Malkin, Jean Pronovost, Mark Recchi, Ulf Samuelsson, Kevin Stevens

HISTORIC MOMENTS

- Mario Lemieux (whose last names translates into English as "the best") is Pittsburgh's all-time leader in seasons (17), games (915), goals (690), assists (1033) and points (1723)

- Won the rights to select Sidney Crosby in a special draft lottery in 2005

ST. LOUIS BLUES

First NHL Season: 1967–68

Star Players: Red Berenson, Bernie Federko, Doug Gilmour, Glenn Hall, Brett Hull, Mike Liut, Al MacInnis, Joe Mullen, Adam Oates, Alex Pietrangelo, Barclay Plager, Jacques Plante, Chris Pronger, Rob Ramage, Brian Sutter, Vladimir Tarasenko, Garry Unger

HISTORIC MOMENTS

- Reached the Stanley Cup Final their first three seasons in the NHL (1967–68 through 1969–70), but got swept each year

Pittsburgh Penguin Sidney Crosby wraps around the net against Los Angeles Kings goalie Jonathan Quick in a game at the Staples Center on November 5, 2009. Crosby scored two goals that game, but the Kings won it 5–2.

LOS ANGELES KINGS

First NHL Season: 1967–68
Star Players: Rob Blake, Dustin Brown, Marcel Dionne, Drew Doughty, Butch Goring, Wayne Gretzky, Kelly Hrudey, Anze Kopitar, Jonathan Quick, Luc Robitaille, Charlie Simmer, Jozef Stumpel, Dave Taylor, Rogie Vachon

HISTORIC MOMENTS

- Acquired Wayne Gretzky in a blockbuster trade with Edmonton on August 9, 1988

- Won their first Stanley Cup in 2011–2012 and became the first team to win the Cup after finishing eighth in their conference

DALLAS STARS (Previously Minnesota North Stars)

First NHL Season: 1967–68
First Season in Dallas: 1993–94
Star Players: Ed Belfour, Brian Bellows, Jamie Benn, Neal Broten, Guy Carbonneau, Dino Ciccarelli, Bill Goldsworthy, Derian Hatcher, Brett Hull, Jere Lehtinen, Cesare Maniago, Gilles Meloche, Mike Modano, Lou Nanne, Joe Nieuwendyk, J. P. Parise, Tyler Seguin, Bobby Smith, Gump Worsley

HISTORIC MOMENTS

- Won five consecutive division titles (1996–97 through 2000–01) in Dallas

- Reached Stanley Cup Final twice in Minnesota (1980–81 and 1990–91)

- Won first Stanley Cup in (1998–99)

BUFFALO SABRES

First NHL Season: 1970–71
Star Players: Dave Andreychuk, Tom Barrasso, Roger Crozier, Jack Eichel, Mike Foligno, Danny Gare, Dominik Hasek, Dale Hawerchuk, Tim Horton, Phil Housley, Pat LaFontaine, Don Luce, Rick Martin, Alexander Mogilny, Michael Peca, Gilbert Perreault, Jason Pominville, Craig Ramsay, René Robert, Jim Schoenfeld

HISTORIC MOMENTS

- Won first pick in the 1970 NHL Entry Draft with a lucky spin of a wheel, and chose future Hall of Famer Gilbert Perreault

- Perreault is the Sabres' all-time leader in games played (1191), goals (512), assists (814) and points (1326)

VANCOUVER CANUCKS

First NHL Season: 1970–71
Star Players: Andre Boudrias, Richard Brodeur, Pavel Bure, Thomas Gradin, Ryan Kesler, Orland Kurtenbach, Don Lever, Trevor Linden, Roberto Luongo, Kirk McLean, Mark Messier, Alexander Mogilny, Markus Naslund, Barry Pederson, Daniel Sedin, Henrik Sedin, Stan Smyl, Harold Snepsts, Dale Tallon, Tony Tanti

Washington Capitals winger Alex Ovechkin leaps between Dan Hamhuis and Daniel Sedin of the Vancouver Canucks during their game at Rogers Arena on October 28, 2013. The Canucks bested the Capitals 3–2. Daniel's twin brother Henrik also played.

HISTORIC MOMENTS

- Team record of 60 goals in a season set by Pavel Bure (1992–93 and 1993–94)

- Brothers Henrik (2009–10) and Daniel Sedin (2010–11) are the only brothers in NHL history to lead the league in scoring in back-to-back seasons

NEW YORK ISLANDERS

First NHL Season: 1972–73
Star Players: Mike Bossy, Bob Bourne, Pat Flatley, Clark Gillies, Butch Goring, Kelly Hrudey, Pat LaFontaine, Bob Nystrom, Zigmund Palffy, Denis Potvin, Chico Resch, Billy Smith, Brent Sutter, John Tavares, John Tonelli, Bryan Trottier

HISTORIC MOMENTS

- Won four straight Stanley Cups from 1979–80 to 1982–83 (since then, no team has won more than two in a row)

- Mike Bossy holds NHL record with nine consecutive 50-goal seasons, from 1977–78 to 1985–86

26

CALGARY FLAMES
(Previously Atlanta Flames)
First NHL Season: 1972–73
First Season in Calgary: 1980–81
Star Players: Dan Bouchard, Guy Chouinard, Theoren Fleury, Johnny Gaudreau, Jarome Iginla, Miikka Kiprusoff, Reggie Lemelin, Hakan Loob, Tom Lysiak, Al MacInnis, Lanny McDonald, Joe Mullen, Joe Nieuwendyk, Kent Nilsson, Jim Peplinksi, Gary Roberts, Gary Suter, Eric Vail, Mike Vernon

HISTORIC MOMENTS

- Single-season record of 66 goals set by Lanny McDonald in 1982–83

- Set team records with 54 wins and 117 points, and won the Stanley Cup, in 1988–89

WASHINGTON CAPITALS
First NHL Season: 1974–75
Star Players: Nicklas Backstrom, Peter Bondra, Dave Christian, Dino Ciccarelli, Mike Gartner, Kevin Hatcher, Braden Holtby, Dale Hunter, Olaf Kolzig, Rod Langway, Dennis Maruk, Larry Murphy, Adam Oates, Alex Ovechkin, Pete Peeters, Mike Ridley, Scott Stevens, Ryan Walter

HISTORIC MOMENTS

- Record of 8–67–5 in first season marked the fewest wins ever for an NHL team in a season of 70 games or more

- Franchise scoring leader Alex Ovechkin scored his 500th career goal on January 10, 2016

NEW JERSEY DEVILS
(Previously Kansas City Scouts and Colorado Rockies)
First NHL Season: 1974–75
First Season in Colorado: 1976–77
First Season in New Jersey: 1982–83
Star Players: Barry Beck, Martin Brodeur, Aaron Broten, Sean Burke, Mike Cammalleri, Bob Carpenter, Ken Daneyko, Patrik Elias, Viacheslav Fetisov, Brian Gionta, Scott Gomez, Bobby Holik, Claude Lemieux, John MacLean, Kirk Muller, Scott Niedermayer, Wilf Paiement, Zach Parise, Rob Ramage, Brendan Shanahan, Scott Stevens, Pat Verbeek

HISTORIC MOMENTS

- First NHL franchise to move cities twice

- Oldest NHL franchise without a 50-goal scorer

- Stanley Cup champions in 1994–95, 1999–2000 and 2002–03

A WHOLE NEW WORLD

When the World Hockey Association (WHA) started in 1972, it marked the first time in many years that the NHL had a rival. No one had really tried to challenge the NHL since the collapse of the Western Hockey League in 1926.

NHL owners didn't take it seriously when the WHA started organizing in 1971, but soon they had no choice. When superstar Bobby Hull left the Chicago Blackhawks to sign with the new league in the summer of 1972, it proved that the WHA meant business. The WHA was offering bigger contracts to its players, and the NHL was forced to pay more money to its own players to keep them happy. At the start of the 1970s, the average salary in the NHL was only $18,000. By the start of the 1980s, it had grown to more than $100,000.

Many players who had never done very well in the NHL became big stars in the WHA. The new league was faster to welcome players from Europe than the NHL had been. It also let Wayne Gretzky play when he was only 17 years old.

Still, it wasn't easy to keep the new league going. Teams jumped around from city to city, sometimes even moving to a new one in the middle of a season. After starting off with 12 teams in 1972–73, the WHA grew to 14 teams two years later, but was down to only six in 1978–79. Over the years there was talk of merging the two leagues, but the NHL was never really interested in that. Finally, during the 1978–79 season, it was announced that the WHA would go out of business at the end of the year. The Edmonton Oilers, New England Whalers, Quebec Nordiques and Winnipeg Jets joined the NHL in 1979–80, pushing the league to 21 teams.

EDMONTON OILERS

Franchise formed: 1972
(as Alberta Oilers)
First NHL Season: 1979–80
Star Players: Glenn Anderson, Paul Coffey, Leon Draisaitl, Jordan Eberle, Grant Fuhr, Wayne Gretzky, Bill Guerin, Charlie Huddy, Jari Kurri, Kevin Lowe, Connor McDavid, Mark Messier, Andy Moog, Ryan Nugent-Hopkins, Bill Ranford, Ryan Smyth, Esa Tikkanen, Doug Weight

HISTORIC MOMENTS

- Reached first Stanley Cup Final in fourth NHL season (1982–83)

- Won Stanley Cup five times in seven years, from 1983–84 through 1989–90

- Hold NHL record for most goals in a single season (446 in 1983–84)

THE BEST EVER?

Every era in NHL history has had its share of great players. But who's the best player ever? Three names top that list. One is Gordie Howe. When it comes to being great for a long time, nobody beats him. Gordie Howe played 25 seasons with the Detroit Red Wings, from 1946–47 to 1970–71. In that time, he led the NHL in scoring six times; he finished in the top three 11 times, in the top five 20 times and in the top ten 21 times. He returned to hockey in 1973 to play in the WHA alongside his sons, Mark and Marty, and was back in the NHL to play one final season in 1979–80 at the age of 51!

Bobby Orr's career was much shorter, but he was pretty great, too. Because of serious injuries to his knees, Orr played less than nine full seasons in 12 years between 1966 and 1979. Even so, no one has ever been a better two-way player than he was. Orr won the Norris Trophy as the NHL's best defenceman for eight straight seasons with the Boston Bruins, from 1967–68 through 1974–75, and he is the only defenceman ever to win the Art Ross Trophy as the league's scoring leader. In fact, he won it twice: in 1969–70 and 1974–75.

Still, when it comes to scoring, no one in the history of hockey has done it better than Wayne Gretzky. Gretzky won the Art Ross Trophy a record 10 times in his 20-year career and won the Hart Trophy as MVP a record nine times. Gretzky set more than 60 scoring records between 1979–80 and 1998–99. Most of those records have yet to be broken, and many of them never will be!

Wayne Gretzky led the Edmonton Oilers to victory over the Boston Bruins in the 1988 Stanley Cup Final. He led the league in both points (43) and assists (31) in that year's playoffs and won the Conn Smythe Trophy.

COLORADO AVALANCHE
(Previously Quebec Nordiques)
Franchise Formed: 1972
First NHL Season: 1979–80
First Season in Colorado: 1995–96
Star Players: Matt Duchene, Adam Foote, Peter Forsberg, Robbie Ftorek, Michel Goulet, Milan Hejduk, Dale Hunter, Uwe Krupp, Gabriel Landeskog, Sylvain Lefebvre, Claude Lemieux, Nathan MacKinnon, Sandis Ozolinsh, Patrick Roy, Joe Sakic, Anton Stastny, Marian Stastny, Peter Stastny, Marc Tardif

HISTORIC MOMENTS

- Hall of Famer Joe Sakic spent his entire 20-year career with the Quebec/Colorado franchise and is its career leader in games (1378), goals (625), assists (1016) and points (1641)

- Set an NHL record with nine straight division titles (1994–95 through 2002–03)

ARIZONA COYOTES
(Previously Winnipeg Jets and Phoenix Coyotes)
Franchise Formed: 1972
First NHL Season: 1979–80
First Season in Phoenix: 1996–97
First Season as Arizona: 2014–15
Star Players: Dave Babych, Shane Doan, Max Domi, Oliver Ekman-Larsson, Dale Hawerchuk, Bobby Hull (WHA), Nikolai Khabibulin, Morris Lukowich, Paul MacLean, Teppo Numminen, Jeremy Roenick, Teemu Selanne, Doug Smail, Mike Smith, Thomas Steen, Keith Tkachuk

HISTORIC MOMENTS

- Set NHL record with 30-game winless streak (23 losses, 7 ties) in 1980–81

- Teemu Selanne set NHL rookie records with 76 goals and 132 points with Winnipeg in 1992–93

- Won first division title in franchise history in Phoenix in 2011–12

CAROLINA HURRICANES
(Previously Hartford Whalers)
Franchise formed: 1972 (as New England Whalers)
First NHL Season: 1979–80
First Season in Carolina: 1997–98
Star Players: Dave Babych, Rod Brind'Amour, John Cullen, Kevin Dineen, Ron Francis, Noah Hanifin, Gordie Howe, Mark Howe, Arturs Irbe, Sami Kapanen, Trevor Kidd, Mike Liut, Jeff O'Neill, Mike Rogers, Jeff Skinner, Eric Staal, Blaine Stoughton, Pat Verbeek, Cam Ward, Glen Wesley

HISTORIC MOMENTS

- Won their first division title in Hartford in 1986–87

- Reached the Stanley Cup Final for the first time in 2001–02

- Won the Stanley Cup in 2005–06

SAN JOSE SHARKS

First NHL Season: 1991–92
Star Players: Dan Boyle, Brent Burns, Jonathan Cheechoo, Logan Couture, Vincent Damphousse, Pat Falloon, Jeff Friesen, Brian Hayward, Martin Jones, Kelly Kisio, Patrick Marleau, Evgeni Nabokov, Owen Nolan, Joe Pavelski, Mike Ricci, Joe Thornton

HISTORIC MOMENTS

- Set an NHL record for most losses by going 11–71–2 in their second season (1992–93)

- Set an NHL record for improvement (58 points) from one season to another by going from 24 points in 1992–93 to 82 points (33–35–16) in 1993–94

- Reached the Stanley Cup Final for the first time in 2016

OTTAWA SENATORS

First NHL Season: 1992–93
Star Players: Daniel Alfredsson, Craig Anderson, Radek Bonk, Mike Fisher, Dany Heatley, Marian Hossa, Erik Karlsson, Brad Marsh, Chris Phillips, Wade Redden, Damian Rhodes, Bobby Ryan, Ron Tugnutt, Alexei Yashin

San Jose Sharks defenceman Brent Burns scores against Ottawa Senators goalie Mike Condon, outgunning Ben Harpur and Erik Karlsson (right) at the Canadian Tire Centre. The Sharks took the game 4–3.

HISTORIC MOMENTS

- Set an NHL record with 38 consecutive road losses during their first season

- Daniel Alfredsson won the Calder Trophy as NHL Rookie of the Year in 1995–96

- Erik Karlsson won the James Norris Trophy for the first time in 2011–12

TAMPA BAY LIGHTNING

First NHL Season: 1992–93
Star Players: Ben Bishop, Dan Boyle, Brian Bradley, Chris Gratton, Roman Hamrlik, Victor Hedman, Nikolai Khabibulin, Chris Kontos, Nikita Kucherov, Vincent Lecavalier, Fredrik Modin, Brad Richards, Steven Stamkos, Martin St. Louis

HISTORIC MOMENTS

- Chris Kontos scored four goals in the first regular-season game in franchise history, in a 7–3 win over Chicago (October 7, 1992)

- Missed playoffs nine times in their first 10 years

- Won first division title in 2002–03 and won the Stanley Cup in 2003–04

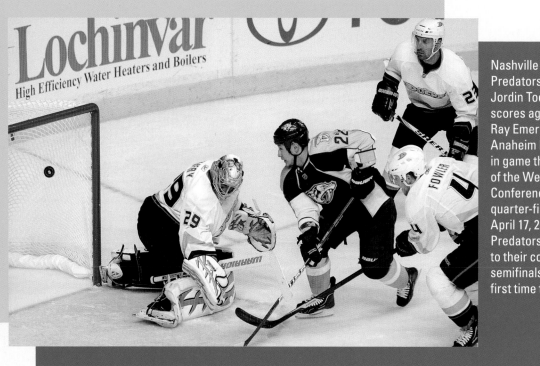

Nashville Predators forward Jordin Tootoo scores against Ray Emery of the Anaheim Ducks in game three of the Western Conference quarter-finals on April 17, 2011. The Predators made it to their conference semifinals for the first time that year.

ANAHEIM DUCKS (Previously Mighty Ducks of Anaheim)

First NHL Season: 1993–94
Star Players: Ryan Getzlaf, Jean-Sebastien Giguere, Guy Hebert, Paul Kariya, Ryan Kesler, Scott Niedermayer, Corey Perry, Steve Rucchin, Ruslan Salei, Teemu Selanne

HISTORIC MOMENTS

- Team was originally owned by The Walt Disney Company and named the Mighty Ducks of Anaheim after the popular 1992 Disney movie *The Mighty Ducks*

- Thirty-three wins in their first season tied the Florida Panthers for the most by a modern expansion team

- Won first division title and Stanley Cup in 2006–07

FLORIDA PANTHERS

First NHL Season: 1993–94
Star Players: Pavel Bure, Brian Campbell, Radek Dvorak, Aaron Ekblad, Jonathan Huberdeau, Jaromir Jagr, Olli Jokinen, Roberto Luongo, Scott Mellanby, Rob Niedermayer, John Vanbiesbrouck, Stephen Weiss

HISTORIC MOMENTS

- Reached Stanley Cup Final in just their third season (1995–96)

- Missed playoffs for an NHL-record 10 straight seasons (2001–02 through 2010–11)

- Won first division title in franchise history (2011–12)

NASHVILLE PREDATORS

First NHL Season: 1998–99
Star Players: Martin Erat, Filip Forsberg, Patric Hornqvist, Greg Johnson, David Legwand, Pekka Rinne, P. K. Subban, Steve Sullivan, Ryan Suter, Kimmo Timonen, Jordin Tootoo, Tomas Vokoun, Shea Weber

HISTORIC MOMENTS

- Admitted as an expansion team on June 25, 1997

- Made their first playoff appearance in 2003–04

- Won their first playoff series in 2010–11

WINNIPEG JETS
(Previously Atlanta Thrashers)

First NHL Season: 1999–2000
First Season in Winnipeg: 2011–12
Star Players: Dustin Byfuglien, Nikolaj Ehlers, Dany Heatley, Marian Hossa, Ilya Kovalchuk, Vyacheslav Kozlov, Andrew Ladd, Patrik Laine, Mark Scheifele, Blake Wheeler

HISTORIC MOMENTS

- Admitted as an expansion team on June 25, 1997

- Won first division title and made first playoff appearance in 2006–07

- Played first game in Winnipeg on October 9, 2011

Columbus Blue Jackets defenceman Jack Johnson and Minnesota Wild center Tyler Graovac battle for the puck during a game on March 2, 2017, at Nationwide Arena. Columbus defeated Minnesota 1–0.

COLUMBUS BLUE JACKETS

First NHL Season: 2000–01
Star Players: Cam Atkinson, Sergei Bobrovsky, Nick Foligno, Sam Gagner, Ryan Johansen, Rostislav Klesla, Steve Mason, Rick Nash, Geoff Sanderson, R. J. Umberger, Zach Werenski, Ray Whitney, Nikolai Zherdev

HISTORIC MOMENTS

- Admitted as an expansion team on June 25, 1997

- In 2003–04, at age 19, Rick Nash tied Jarome Iginla and Ilya Kovalchuk for the NHL lead with 41 goals, making him the youngest player in history to lead the NHL in goals

- Goalie Sergei Bobrovsky became the first Russian to win the Vezina Trophy (2012–13)

MINNESOTA WILD

First NHL Season: 2000–01
Star Players: Niklas Backstrom, Pierre-Marc Bouchard, Andrew Brunette, Cal Clutterbuck, Devan Dubnyk, Manny Fernandez, Marian Gaborik, Mikko Koivu, Zach Parise, Dwayne Roloson, Brian Rolston, Nick Schultz, Ryan Suter, Wes Walz

HISTORIC MOMENTS

- Admitted as an expansion team on June 25, 1997

- Set an expansion-team record for attendance in their first season and continued to sell out every home game during their first 10 seasons, 409 games in all

VEGAS GOLDEN KNIGHTS

First NHL Season: 2017–18

HISTORIC MOMENTS

- Expansion team awarded to Las Vegas on June 22, 2016

- Team name announced on November 22, 2016

RULES OF THE GAME

THE HALIFAX RULES

The earliest hockey rules are believed to have been drawn up in Nova Scotia around the mid-1800s. They were never actually written down at the time, but an old–time player from the Dartmouth area explained the rules to a reporter in 1879. These early rules have become known as "The Halifax Rules."

- The game was played with a block of wood for a puck.
- The puck was not allowed to leave the ice.
- The stones marking the place to score goals were placed on the ice (at right angles to those at present) parallel to the sides of the ice surface.
- There was to be no slashing.
- There was to be no lifting the stick above the shoulder.
- When a goal was scored, teams changed ends.

- Players had to keep "on side" of the puck.
- The "forward pass" was permitted.
- All players played the entire game.
- There was a no-replacement rule for penalized players.
- The game had two 30-minute periods with a 10-minute break.
- The goalkeeper had to stand for the entire game.
- Goals were decided by the goal umpires, who stood at the goal mouth and rang a handbell.

THE MONTREAL RULES

The rules written down by James Creighton and his friends at McGill University in Montreal in 1877 have many similarities to the Halifax Rules. One key difference was that the rules in Montreal did not allow forward passing. This may have been because the Montreal Rules were based on the rules of field hockey, which still does not allow forward passing. Here are those early Montreal Rules:

- The game will begin and be continued with a faceoff at centre. Teams will change ends after each goal.
- When a player shoots the puck, anyone on the same team who is closer to the opponent's goal is out of play (offside) and may not touch the puck until it has been played by someone else. A player must always be on his own side of the puck.
- The puck may be stopped, but cannot be carried or shot by any part of the body. No player shall raise his stick above his shoulder. Charging from behind, tripping, collaring, kicking or shinning is not allowed.

- When the attacking team has shot the puck off of the ice behind the goal line, it shall be brought back 15 yards (13.7 metres) and play started again by a faceoff. If the defending team shoots it out, a player from the attacking team will be given possession within one yard (.9 metres) of the nearest corner.
- When the puck goes off at the side, a player from the other team shall roll it back into play.
- If any of the above rules are broken, play will restart with a faceoff.
- All disputes will be settled by the umpire or the referee.

Players who broke the rules in these early days weren't sent off the ice like they are today for penalties. The only thing that happened was that play was stopped and restarted with a faceoff. But in those days, they didn't call it a faceoff, they called it a "bully." And the referee didn't drop the puck like they do today. The puck was placed between two players, who tapped their sticks on the ice and against each other's three times before scrambling to whack the puck.

WRITING THE RULES

James George Aylwin Creighton is credited as the man who wrote the rules of hockey that appeared in the *Montreal Gazette* back in 1877. Born and raised in Halifax, Nova Scotia, Creighton moved to Montreal in 1872. Shortly after arriving, he and some friends tried to play a game of lacrosse on ice at the Victoria Skating Rink. That didn't work out so well. So Creighton decided to get some hockey sticks from back home and teach his friends the game that had been played for years in Nova Scotia. That was the beginning of the game of hockey as we know it today.

THE NATIONAL HOCKEY LEAGUE

DUTIES *of* OFFICIALS *and* LAWS *of* HOCKEY

Adopted November 26th, 1917

The National Hockey League was founded in 1917. This is the original rule book.

IN THE CREASE

The earliest known printed rules of hockey appeared in the Montreal Gazette. *However, they didn't mention anything about the size of the ice. The first known rule book to mention dimensions is one put together by the Spalding Sporting Goods company. In their Ice Hockey and Ice Polo Guide 1898, it says the rink "shall be at least 112 feet by 58 feet."*

THE RINK

Rule 1 in the *Official NHL Rulebook* is simply called "Rink." The rule begins just as simply, too: "National Hockey League games shall be played on an ice surface known as the 'Rink.'" It gets a little more complicated after that, adding that the Rink "must adhere to the dimensions and specifications prescribed by the League and these rules." There are then eight more parts to the rule, describing the boards, glass, netting and all the lines, dots and circles on the ice (see Official NHL Rink Dimensions, page 122). Rule 1.2 states that the official size of the rink will be 200 feet long and 85 feet wide. Those dimensions have been listed in the rulebook since the 1929–30 season.

They are almost exactly the same size as the ice surface at the Victoria Skating Rink in Montreal, where hockey was first played indoors.

PLAY YOUR POSITION

When hockey first started outdoors on frozen ponds and rivers, there didn't really have to be rules about how many people could play. There was usually room for as many players as showed up. But when hockey moved to indoor rinks, there was only so much space available. As the modern game got going in the 1870s, there were usually nine players on the ice per team: a goalie, four forwards and four defencemen. Similar to rugby and field hockey, the defencemen were known as backs and halfbacks.

In a pickup game, the rink can be any size and there can be any number of players. Pictured here are players on a public rink by the St. Clair streetcar barns in Toronto, 1915.

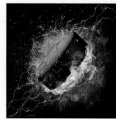
During the 1880s, hockey teams were reduced to seven players. They played the game with three forwards, two halfbacks, a back and a goalie. But things changed again in the 1890s. By 1892, there were four forwards on the ice and only two defencemen, but the defencemen were called the point and cover point. Instead of lining up beside each other as defencemen do today, the point man lined up in front of his goalie, with the cover point in a straight line a little bit farther up the ice. It was around 1914 that defencemen started to play beside each other and the terms "point" and "cover point" began to disappear. The fourth forward was known as the rover.

Back in those days, players were expected to remain on the ice for the full 60 minutes of the game. Substitutes off the bench were used very rarely, and only when there was a serious injury. To play the full 60 minutes, players had to pace themselves. As a result, defencemen usually concentrated their efforts on their team's end of the ice, while the forwards tried to score goals at the other end. The rover had more of a free hand and could help the team's defencemen protect their goalie or help the forwards on offense.

The National Hockey Association dropped the rover during the 1911–12 season. Other amateur leagues soon followed suit, but the Pacific Coast Hockey Association — even though it introduced so many other modern rules — didn't drop the seventh player until the 1922–23 season. By then, the era of the rover was completely over.

RULES AND RULE CHANGES

Passing the Puck

Aside from there being seven players on the ice instead of six, the biggest difference between the game then and now was that no real forward passing was allowed. Players could drop the puck back to a teammate, or shoot it all the way to the other end and chase after it. They could make short passes a little ways in front of them, but the only players allowed to receive the puck were players that had been behind the passer to begin with. The best way to advance with the puck was by skating and stickhandling.

The first major hockey league to introduce forward passing was the Pacific Coast Hockey Association. At the start of the 1913–14 season, the PCHA painted the first blue lines on the ice and allowed players to pass the puck to a player ahead of them when they were all in the neutral zone. The NHL did not allow forward passing during its first season in 1917–18, but did permit it in the neutral zone after adding the blue lines in 1918–19. Forward passing made hockey move a lot faster, but people didn't want the game to speed up too much. It took until the 1929–30 season before the NHL allowed forward passing everywhere on the ice. And there was still a catch: players weren't allowed to pass across either blue line, so the puck still had to be carried from zone to zone. Soon, teams were clogging up the blue lines and the game slowed down again.

In the 1943–44 season, the NHL added the centre ice red line in order to help speed things up again. Teams were now allowed to pass the puck across their own blue line, as long as they didn't pass it across centre ice. It took until the 2005–06 season to change the rules again so that teams could pass the puck out of their own zone, across centre, and all the way up to the other team's blue line. These long passes are often called "stretch" passes and have helped make hockey faster than ever. Some people wonder if it's now too fast!

Faceoffs

Faceoffs in the early days of hockey were still a bit different than they are today. Until the early 1900s, the referee would place the puck on the ice between the sticks of the two centers and then shout, "Play!" This is similar to the way faceoffs are still done in lacrosse today, but the results of these faceoffs in old-time hockey were a lot of bruised knuckles for the referees. Fred Waghorne, who is a member of the Hockey Hall of Fame, is believed to have been the first referee to drop the puck on faceoffs.

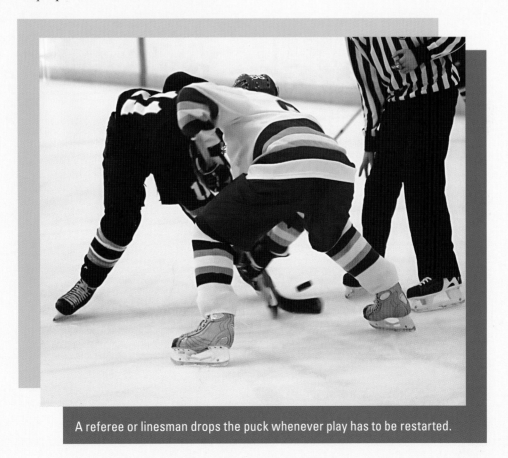

A referee or linesman drops the puck whenever play has to be restarted.

Icing and Other Delays

When players had to play the full 60 minutes of a game, they could get pretty worn out.

Every so often, they might flip the puck into the stands just to get a quick break. But they wouldn't get a penalty for delaying the game.

There was no rule against icing the puck, either. In fact, in the days before forward passing, icing the puck could be strategic: you had to give up possession to the other team, but at least it got you out of trouble in your own end. A long, high "loft shot" down to the other end of the ice was a skill every good defenceman needed.

Even after forward passing was instituted, there was still no rule against icing for several years. It became a strategy for teams to try to take an early lead in the game and then fire the puck down the ice as often as possible to try and protect it. The strategy was effective — but not a lot of fun for the fans in attendance!

Finally, on September 24, 1937, the NHL passed a rule against icing. From then on, if a team shot the puck down the ice from its own end, play would be stopped and the puck would be brought back for a faceoff. Teams were still allowed to ice the puck without a whistle if they had a penalty, and that remains part of the icing rules to this day.

PENALTIES

On January 8, 1886, the sports page in the *Montreal Gazette* printed a brand new set of hockey rules. They were pretty similar to the rules of 1877, but now there would be a worse punishment for breaking the rules than just a faceoff. This time, the rules said, "after being warned twice by the referee, it shall become his duty to rule the player off the ice for the [rest of the game]."

For the next few years, the only kind of penalty was to kick a player out of the game, a match penalty. Around 1904, referees were also given the option of sending a player off the ice for two, three

A referee calls a slashing penalty.

or five minutes. When the NHL began in 1917–18, there were three-minute penalties and five-minute penalties in addition to match penalties. Referees could also fine the players set amounts of money. Penalties had definitely gotten stricter, but teams never actually had to play shorthanded. Any time a player got a penalty, someone else was allowed to come on to replace him. That rule was changed for the 1918–19 season. Ever since then, teams have had to play shorthanded if they have someone in the penalty box. Three-minute penalties were reduced to two minutes in 1921–22.

Minor Penalties

A player receives a minor penalty when he does something that's against the rules but isn't so serious. A minor penalty is two minutes long, though sometimes a player will receive a "double minor" and have to sit in the penalty box for four minutes. A player serving a minor penalty is allowed to return to the ice early if his team gives up a goal while they are shorthanded. That wasn't always the case. Until the 1956–57 season, teams had to play shorthanded for a full two minutes no matter how many power-play goals the other team scored.

Major Penalties

Major penalties are five minutes long. They are given out for more serious infractions. Fighting is always a five-minute major, and most penalties that are usually minors (such as slashing, elbowing or hooking) can be bumped up to a five-minute major if the referee thinks the play was too violent or the player broke the rules on purpose. Players

serving a major penalty stay in the box for the full five minutes no matter how many power-play goals the other team scores. Any player receiving three major penalties in one game gets kicked out for the rest of the game.

Misconducts

Misconduct penalties were first introduced to the NHL rulebook for the 1937–38 season. These penalties are usually called when tempers get out of hand or when a player or a coach is verbally abusive toward a referee. Misconduct penalties are 10 minutes long, though there are also game misconducts that see the player kicked out for the rest of the game, no matter how much time is left. Teams do not have to play shorthanded during a misconduct penalty, though often there is a two-minute minor penalty involved as well.

Match Penalties

A match penalty is given out to any player who deliberately injures an opponent, or who the referee thinks has tried to injure an opposing player on purpose. A player is kicked out for the rest of the game and cannot play again until the league commissioner has reviewed the case. When a player receives a match penalty, his team has to put another player in the penalty box and play shorthanded for five minutes.

Penalty Shot

Penalty shots were first introduced in the Pacific Coast Hockey Association in 1921–22. They were not added to the NHL rulebook until the 1934–35 season. Originally, a penalty shot was only awarded when a player on a breakaway was tripped before he could shoot the puck.

In the early days, players weren't allowed to skate right in on the goalie for a penalty shot like they do today. They had to shoot from a fixed spot on the ice. That part of the rule was changed in 1945.

Goalies and Penalties

In the early days of the NHL, goalies had to sit in the penalty box like any other player if they broke the rules. Teams only carried one goalie on their roster, so a forward or a defenceman would have to take over in net. Rules about goalies and penalties were changed a lot during the 1930s and 1940s. Sometimes another player was allowed to serve the penalty instead, or sometimes the other team would be awarded a penalty shot. Since the 1949–50 season, a teammate has always been allowed to serve the penalty if a minor or a major is called against a goalie. A teammate will also serve a 10-minute misconduct given to a goalie, but if a goalie receives a game misconduct or a match penalty, the goalie is kicked out of the game. If, for any reason, no back-up goalie is available, another teammate is allowed to put on the goalie's equipment and go in the net.

Other Penalty Notes

A team can never be forced to play more than two men short at one time. If a third penalty is called while a team already has two men in the penalty box, that player has to go directly to the penalty box, but his penalty time will not start until the penalty of one of the two other players has expired.

Also, if a minor penalty is going to be called on a team and the other team scores a goal before the referee blows his whistle to stop the play, the penalty is wiped out. If the same thing happens before a major or match penalty can be called, the penalty counts and the team still has to play shorthanded.

HERE ARE THE NINE REASONS IN THE CURRENT NHL RULEBOOK FOR A PENALTY SHOT TO BE CALLED

1. Deliberate illegal substitution.
2. Intentionally dislodging the net during a breakaway.
3. Intentionally dislodging the net when the delay of game penalty cannot be fully served within regulation time.
4. Falling on the puck in the goal crease.
5. Picking up the puck by hand in the goal crease.
6. Player on a breakaway is interfered with by an opposing player throwing an object.
7. Player on a breakaway is interfered with by an opposing player who has entered the game illegally.
8. Player or goalie throws or shoots an object at the puck in his zone.
9. Player on a breakaway is fouled from behind.

PENALTIES

Boarding: Pushing or checking a player in such a way that the opponent hits the boards violently or dangerously.

Butt-ending: Hitting an opponent with the shaft of the stick above the upper hand.

Charging: Skating or jumping at a player in a violent manner after skating a distance to reach the opponent.

Checking from behind: A check delivered to a player who cannot defend himself because he could not see the checker coming.

Clipping: A check delivered to a player below the knees.

Cross-checking: Using the shaft of the stick between the two hands to hit an opponent.

Diving: When a player falls on purpose, or exaggerates falling down, or pretends to be injured to try and get the referee to call a penalty on an opposing player.

Elbowing: Hitting an opponent with an extended elbow.

Fighting: When at least one player punches or attempts to punch an opponent repeatedly, or when two players wrestle in a way that makes it difficult for the linesmen to separate them.

PENALTIES

Head-butting: Hitting an opponent, or even trying to hit an opponent, by leading with the head or helmet.

High-sticking: Hitting an opponent with a stick carried above the height of the opponent's shoulder.

Holding: Any action by a player to grab or try and slow down an opponent.

Holding the stick: A player is not permitted to hold an opponent's stick.

Hooking: Using the stick to slow down an opponent.

Illegal check to the head: A hit resulting in contact with a player's head where the head was the main point of contact.

Interference: Impeding the progress of a player who is not in possession of the puck.

Instigator: A player who is first to start a fight.

Kicking: Deliberately using a skate with a kicking motion to contact an opponent.

Kneeing: Leading with the knee, or extending the leg outward, when making a check.

PENALTIES

Roughing: Pushing or shoving after a whistle has been blown, or when it takes place away from the play.

Slashing: Swinging a stick at an opponent, whether contact is made or not.

Slew-footing: Using a leg or foot to knock or kick an opponent's feet from under him.

Spearing: Jabbing an opponent with the point of the stick blade, whether any contact is made or not.

Throwing equipment: A player throws his stick or any other piece of equipment in towards the puck or an opponent.

Too many men on the ice: Having more than six players on the ice, if not already shorthanded.

Tripping: Purposefully causing an opponent to fall. No penalty will be called if a player made contact with the puck before the fall.

Unsportsmanlike conduct: Actions such as abusive language, biting, hair-pulling, or throwing objects onto the ice from the bench.

HOCKEY GEAR

STICK WITH IT

When people started playing hockey in Canada around the early 1800s, they most likely used sticks from the Irish game of hurling. People who didn't have a hurley might have cut their own sticks from tree branches.

By the start of the 1900s, the best hockey sticks were made by the Mi'kmaq in Nova Scotia. They carved their sticks from the lower part of a tree, including the roots, where the wood was strongest. Yellow birch and hornbeam were the trees they preferred. Mi'kmaq sticks were solid and sturdy and could last a player for many years. The sticks weren't very flexible, however, so it was hard to get much power behind a shot or lift the puck off the ice.

Over the years, other people who made hockey sticks experimented with different types of wood. They used rock elm, white ash and hickory to make lighter, more flexible sticks. A big breakthrough came from a company in St. Marys, Ontario, in the 1920s. Instead of making its sticks

THEN AND NOW: STICKS

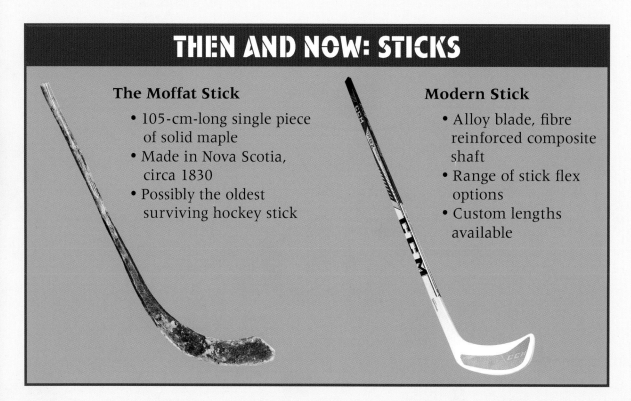

The Moffat Stick
- 105-cm-long single piece of solid maple
- Made in Nova Scotia, circa 1830
- Possibly the oldest surviving hockey stick

Modern Stick
- Alloy blade, fibre reinforced composite shaft
- Range of stick flex options
- Custom lengths available

from one piece of wood, it made the shaft from one piece and the blade from another. The two pieces were then wedged together and held with strong glue.

Pretty much all hockey sticks were made of wood until the 1970s. Fibreglass blades on wooden sticks were introduced around 1976. Shafts made of aluminum were introduced in 1979 and approved for use in the NHL in 1981. In more recent years, composite sticks have become popular. These sticks are made from two or more different materials. Fibreglass is still used, but so are other materials such as graphite, Kevlar and titanium. Players loved the light weight and flexibility of these new sticks, but the earlier versions were easy to break. New technology has made these sticks more durable with even more flexibility and a larger "sweet spot" on the blade for even more powerful shots.

Tape

Players have been taping their sticks since at least the early 1900s. But why? Solid old sticks may have lasted for years, but they tended to splinter and crack. Tape helped with that. Then as now, though, the main reason for tape was to help with the grip, both that a player gets on his or her stick and that the stick gets on the puck. In fact, NHL rule 10.1 says that tape "may be wrapped around the stick at any place for the purpose of reinforcement or to improve control of the puck." The rule also says that tape of any colour can be used, but many players think using black tape on the blade makes it a bit more difficult for the goalie to see the puck.

Rule 10.2 says that goalies must have a knob at the top of their sticks, and that it must be made of "white tape or some other protective material approved by the league." The knob has to be white so that it won't be confused with the puck if it ends up in the net!

Bending the Blade

Early hockey sticks had straight blades. One of the first players to experiment with a curved one was Cy Denneny, a future Hall of Famer who played with the original Ottawa Senators in the NHA and the NHL in the 1910s and 1920s. Denneny would dip the blade of his stick into boiling water until it softened, and then bend it a bit before it cooled.

Bending the blade made shots more powerful and made the puck move unpredictably. But it also made it harder for the player to stickhandle, or to take shots or make passes on the backhand, so the curved blade didn't catch on. Andy Bathgate, another future Hall of Famer, experimented with curving his blade while growing up in Winnipeg in the 1940s. When he reached the NHL in the 1950s, his coach with the New York Rangers hated his curved sticks. He would break the blades whenever he saw them.

Stan Mikita had more luck with his coach in Chicago in the 1960s. When Mikita and his Blackhawks teammate Bobby Hull began terrifying goalies with powerful slapshots from their curved blades, others players started curving their blades, too. Soon hockey stick companies began making their sticks with curved blades. Today, it's rare to find a hockey player at any level of the game who uses a stick with a straight blade.

Skates

It's believed that skating first got its start around 5000 years ago. The earliest skate blades were made from the leg bones of large animals.

The first skates with metal blades emerged in Holland in the 1500s. There are many paintings from Holland in the 1500s and 1600s showing people on skates. Some of them show skaters carrying sticks and playing a game that looks like it could be hockey. They are probably playing a Dutch game called "kolven" which was similar to golf played on ice.

Early skates used for hockey had blades that simply strapped on to a pair of boots or shoes. By the 1860s, blades were attached with a mechanical lever that made for a much tighter fit. This made stops, starts and turns on the ice a lot easier.

In 1905, Joe Hall was at the start of a career that would see him wind up in the Hockey Hall of Fame. He had a neighbour named George Tackaberry who made shoes. Hall asked him if he would help him improve his hockey skates. Tackaberry used kangaroo leather to make boots that fit more snugly to Hall's feet. He also reinforced the leather to provide better protection in the heel and toe. Tackaberry's new skates — which were known as Tacks — became hugely popular among hockey players.

Today, Tacks are made by CCM and are the most popular skates with NHL players. They can be custom fit to every player, providing both protection and comfort to help generate maximum power.

Hockey Gloves

Early hockey gloves looked a lot like today's gardening gloves. It wasn't until the early 1900s that players began to wear padded leather gloves. The padding was usually provided by felt or animal hair. Many gloves also included thin sticks

THEN AND NOW: SKATES

Skate Blades, 1820s

- Attached to shoes or boots
- Straight, long blades for speed
- Nova Scotia's Starr company was world-famous

Modern Skates

- One-piece boot maximizes energy transfer and provides support
- Curved blades for quick manoeuvres
- CCM Super Tacks are used by most NHL players

made from various types of wood, to give added protection to the wrists and forearms.

Though more modern materials would later be used, hockey gloves in the 1980s didn't look too different from the leather gloves of the 1930s. By the late 1980s and early 1990s, players wanted shorter cuffs on their gloves. They felt that these smaller gloves allowed them to handle the puck better. Today, hockey gloves barely cover more than a player's hand and wrist. Elbow pads have been extended to give more protection to the forearm.

Protecting Shins and Knees

Players began wearing specially designed equipment to protect their shins from sticks and pucks sometime in the 1880s. They used pads made from leather or felt, reinforced with strips of cane (woody pieces of plant stems).

Unlike today, when hockey shin pads come right up over a player's knees, early shin pads were designed to protect only their shins. Knee pads came later. They were made from large squares of leather or canvas strengthened with layers of felt. Some players wore their knee pads on the outside of their hockey socks. It wasn't until the 1920s that shin pads and knee pads were combined into one piece of equipment. When plastic became more readily available in the 1940s, after the end of World War II, shin pads became more effective at protecting against injuries. Later inventions, such as nylon and Velcro, led to even better equipment to protect shins and knees, as well as shoulders and elbows.

Elbows and Shoulders

Some sources say that hockey players began wearing elbow pads as early as 1910. Others say it was as late as 1930. The difference may be that early elbow

THEN AND NOW: GLOVES

Gloves, 1920s
- Padded with animal hair or felt
- Sometimes reinforced with bamboo
- Longer to cover wrists

Modern Gloves
- Lightweight man-made materials
- Shorter for easier stick-handling
- Team colours since the 1950s

pads — which were simply elastic bandages strengthened with felt — were just skinny bits of protection worn under the sleeves of hockey jerseys. By the 1930s, leather elbow pads had become much larger and were beginning to look a little like hot dog buns.

As elbow pads got bigger, many players began wearing them on the outside of their sweaters. Some elbow pads even had metal in them, but the NHL banned pads made of metal in 1937. Before the 1945–46 season, the NHL passed a rule that said all equipment (except helmets, gloves and goalie pads) had to be worn underneath a player's uniform. Even so, elbow pads and shoulder pads were soon being made of such hard plastic that people worried they were causing as many injuries as they prevented. During the 1950s, new rules were passed that elbow pads and shoulder pads had to have a soft outer covering.

Like most other hockey equipment, early shoulder pads were made mostly of felt and leather. Shoulder pads remained pretty skimpy right through the 1970s, with little more than a plastic cap over the shoulder and a bit of other material to cover the chest. These days, as materials have gotten stronger and lighter, shoulder pads have grown to give better protection to the shoulders, chest, ribs and spine.

History of the Helmet

It is believed that George Owen was the first NHL player to wear a helmet. Born in Hamilton, Ontario, Owen grew up in Boston. In 1929, he became the first local player to join the Bruins. Many say that he wore a leather football helmet — probably from his days of playing football at Harvard — during his rookie season with the Bruins.

Following the career-ending head injury to Ace Bailey during the 1933–34 season, some players began to wear helmets. Still, they remained unpopular with NHL players. After Bill Masterton died of a head injury in 1968, several NHL players started wearing helmets. But most players didn't wear them until well into the 1970s.

During the 1970s, rules were passed making helmets mandatory in junior leagues and the college ranks. Many of these players kept their helmets on when they reached the NHL. So did the players who joined the NHL from Europe, where they had always worn them. Finally, in August 1979, the NHL passed a rule making helmets mandatory. However, anyone who had signed a contract before June 1, 1979, didn't have to wear one if he didn't want to. By the 1995–96 season, Craig MacTavish was the last player left in the NHL who wasn't wearing a helmet. He retired the following season.

With so much concern about concussions in sports, today's helmets feature strong, lightweight outer shells with smart foam technology inside that reacts differently to various levels of impact.

Goalie Pads

In the early days of hockey, goaltenders wore the exact same equipment as everybody else on the ice. Even their sticks were the same. One of the earliest stories of a goalie wearing special pads on his legs dates back to 1889 in Dartmouth, Nova Scotia. By 1893, some goalies in Manitoba and Ontario were wearing cricket pads too, but they still weren't common in Montreal — the country's biggest and most important city. On February 14, 1896, goalie George "Whitey" Merritt wore cricket pads when his Winnipeg Victorias played a challenge match for the Stanley Cup against the Montreal Victorias. The Montreal team protested, but Merritt was allowed to wear his pads and he blanked Montreal for a 2–0 Winnipeg victory. His success that night was a big reason why other goalies started wearing pads.

Cricket pads made from leather and cane remained popular for hockey goalies until the 1920s.

During the 1923–24 season, Emil "Pop" Kenesky of Hamilton, Ontario, redesigned the pads worn by Jake Forbes of the local NHL team, the Hamilton Tigers. Cricket pads tended to be narrow and wrap around a goalie's legs. Kenesky used the tools from his job as a harness maker to make Forbes's goalie pads wider

THEN AND NOW: GOALIE GEAR

Georges Vezina, Montreal Canadiens Goalie, 1925

- Specialized goalie pads evolved as an improvement on cricket pads
- Leg guard rule established 1937 — no wider than 10 inches (25.4 cm)
- Glove padding rule established 1958 — no longer than 8 inches (20.3 cm)

Carey Price, Montreal Canadiens Goalie, 2015

- Catcher's mitt-style glove
- NHL has complex rules governing pad size, with a formula that takes into account a player's size
- Maximum leg pad height is 38 inches (96.5 cm)
- Knee pads maximum 9 inches (22.9 cm) long, leg guards 11 inches (27.9 cm) wide

and flatter, jutting out farther to the sides of his legs. Kenesky's pads were leather in front with felt in the back and stuffed thick with kapok (a silky fibre from tropical plants) and deer hair.

Pop Kenesky and his family would continue to make the top goalie pads in hockey until well into the 1980s. By the 1990s, new designs by other companies featuring nylon and foam made goalie pads much lighter, and leather pads like Kenesky's became a thing of the past.

Goalie Sticks

Though Whitey Merritt wasn't the first to wear goalie pads, he may have been the first goalie to use an extra-wide stick.

A team picture of the Winnipeg Victorias from about 1895 shows that Merritt had attached an extra piece of wood to the bottom of his stick. By 1911, the team picture of the Stanley Cup champion Ottawa Senators shows Percy LeSueur with a goalie stick that resembles the type of stick still used today. In 1921, the NHL passed a rule saying that the thick part (often referred to as the "paddle") of a goalie's stick could not be more than 3.5 inches (8.9 cm) in width. That rule is still in the books today. The rule book also says that the paddle cannot extend more than 26 inches (66 cm) up the shaft of the stick.

Goalie Gloves

Around 1910, Ottawa goalie Percy LeSueur designed gloves with longer cuffs to better protect his forearms. Right through the 1920s, goalie gloves remained similar to those worn by other players, but with more felt and leather padding. During the 1930s,

Chicago goalie Mike Karakas introduced a more rounded glove with a webbed pocket between the thumb and index finger.

During the 1946–47 season, Emile Francis, another Blackhawks goalie, asked a team trainer to attach a first-baseman's glove to the cuff of a hockey glove. Other teams weren't happy, but Francis insisted that he be allowed to use his new glove. NHL president Clarence Campbell agreed with him. Within a month, sporting goods companies started making their own versions. All modern catching gloves are just improvements on Francis's original hockey-baseball idea.

Boston's Frank Brimsek was the first goalie to wear a blocker on his stick hand. Brimsek, who starred with the Bruins in the 1930s and 1940s, built a bamboo ribbing over a regular glove. Later, blockers would feature extra padding made of sponge or rubber. They looked a lot like boxing gloves and made it almost impossible to control rebounds.

The next innovation was a solid, rectangular piece of leather that gave the blocker a more modern look. By the mid-1950s, flat surfaces made of wood, and then plastic, began to appear under a cover of leather on the front of blockers.

Bodies and Arms

In the early days of hockey, players couldn't really lift the puck with the solid sticks they used, and goalies had to remain standing at all times, so there wasn't a need for chest protectors. But once the PCHA and the NHL allowed goalies to fall to the ice, it became obvious that goalies needed better protection. So they started wearing chest protectors — or belly pads, as most goalies called them — that were very similar to what baseball catchers used. These were made of leather, canvas and felt. Soon, goalies also added arm pads that they wore like thick felt sleeves under their hockey sweaters.

Even with this new equipment, goalies suffered all sorts of welts and bruises on their upper bodies. Big changes finally came in the 1990s. Protection for the shoulders, chest, stomach and arms were combined into one large piece of equipment. Modern materials made this new "body armour" much stronger and lighter. This allowed goalies to play more of the game lower to the ice without having to worry about getting injured.

Masked Men . . . and Woman

It might be hard to believe, but there was a time when goalies stared down oncoming pucks barefaced. This was true for a very long time!

One of the earliest stories of a hockey mask being used goes back to 1903. After Eddie Giroux of the Toronto Marlboros was injured in a pre-season practice, he returned to the ice a few days later wearing a catcher's mask. He didn't like it and never wore it in a game.

As early as 1912, there were newspaper reports that the NHA planned "to bring up the question of face protection for the goalkeeper." But nothing seemed to come of it. There are a few stories about goalies who played in amateur leagues in Canada and the United States during the 1910s wearing baseball catcher's masks. In 1920, the OHA allowed goalies to wear masks for protection. Still, it seems that none of them did.

On February 7, 1927, goalie Elizabeth Graham of the women's hockey team at Queen's University in Kingston, Ontario, played a game wearing a fencing mask.

THEN AND NOW: GOALIE MASKS

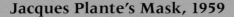

Jacques Plante's Mask, 1959

- Moulded fibreglass, custom fit for a goalie's face
- Held on by straps around the top and back of the head
- Puck difficult to see and track from some angles
- No padding: if a player took a puck to the face, there was often still bruising and swelling

Curtis Joseph's Mask, 2008

- Moulded profile allows a goalie's face to sit closer to the cage, enabling better peripheral vision
- Foam liner and chin cup support help mask feel lighter and provide protection
- Carbon and Kevlar composite shell
- Titanium cage

Apparently it was Elizabeth's father who insisted she wear the mask after he had paid for some expensive dental work.

Three years later, an NHL goalie wore a mask in a game for the very first time. Clint Benedict was a future Hall of Famer playing with the Montreal Maroons. The long-time veteran was hit in the face with shots in back-to-back games on January 4 and January 7, 1930. The second shot broke his nose, and Benedict was sidelined for six weeks. When he returned on February 20, he wore a leather mask. Benedict wore it for five games. Unfortunately, on the night of March 4, 1930, an Ottawa player fell on Benedict in a goalmouth scramble. His mask pushed down on his face . . . and broke his nose again! Benedict never played another NHL game.

The Masked Marvel

During the 1950s, some NHL goalies wore Plexiglas masks in practices. However, these masks fogged up so easily that no one could wear them in a game.

It would be Jacques Plante of the Montreal Canadiens who would make goalie masks famous. Plante wasn't like other goalies. He was one of the first to roam from his crease to get loose pucks. He stopped dump-ins behind the net, and sometimes raced out almost as far as the blue line to pass the puck to his defencemen. After surgery on his face during the 1957–58 season, Plante began wearing a mask in practice.

Soon he was experimenting with new materials to design a better mask. By the start of the 1959–60 season, Plante had an unbreakable mask built by a Montreal company called Fiberglas Canada. Plante's new mask was light, tight and fit just right. Still, Montreal management didn't want him wearing it in games.

By this time, Plante had a long list of injuries. He had fractured each of his cheekbones once. He had broken his nose twice. He'd also had about 150 stitches to fix up all the cuts on his face. For a goalie in those days, this was nothing unusual. Plante might have even considered himself lucky. The unlucky goalies were the ones whose careers ended after they got hit in the eye.

Then, on November 1, 1959, Plante was cut in the face by a shot from Andy Bathgate of the New York Rangers. Teams only had one goalie, so Plante had to get stitched up and go back into the game. However, he refused to return unless Canadiens coach Toe Blake let him wear his mask. Plante wore his mask and soon goalies everywhere followed.

Today, most goalies wear masks that are a combination of a fibreglass shield and small metal bars. The metal "cage" gives better protection to the eyes, because the cage sits farther away from the face, while the more rounded fibreglass part allows pucks to be deflected away safely, with the goalie feeling much less of an impact.

SO YOU WANT TO PLAY

MINOR HOCKEY HISTORY

In the earliest days of hockey history, children learned to play the game on their own on frozen lakes and rivers. Kids got together, picked their own teams, and developed their skills by trial and error. Generations of Canadians learned to play the game this way, even after leagues for young hockey players were established.

As early as the 1890s, some teams at the highest levels of hockey offered programs for children, too. Still, it was mostly schools or church groups that ran organized hockey for kids. By the 1910s, there were leagues with "juvenile" or "midget" teams for teenage boys. Bantam hockey got its start around the 1920s.

MINOR HOCKEY TODAY

These days, players get drafted into the NHL from teams in Europe, American universities and sometimes American high schools. Still, most players drafted into the NHL come from junior teams in Canada. The major junior leagues

Outdoor games of shinny are a Canadian tradition.

are the Ontario Hockey League, the Western Hockey League and the Quebec Major Junior Hockey League. But no matter where players come from, every one of them gets their start playing some form of youth, or minor, hockey.

In Canada, there are different levels of competition for every age group of minor hockey. The beginning level is house league. In house league hockey, teams all come from the same area, and players may be of any skill level. No tryouts are necessary to make a team. Just above house league, there are often select teams. These are like all-star teams for the best house league players.

To play above house league, players have to try out for more competitive teams. These more competitive levels of minor hockey usually involve teams spread out over a wider area and often require lots of travel. Though organizations are different in different parts of Canada, there are often three tiers of competition at the higher levels of youth hockey, beginning with A and moving up to AA and AAA.

In many minor hockey leagues across the country, the atom, pee-wee, bantam and midget categories are split in half, with the younger age group playing Minor Atom, Minor Pee-Wee, and so on. In parts of Canada, players can move on to play junior hockey when they are 15 or 16 years old, but most junior players are aged 18 to 21. Some minor hockey leagues have a juvenile division for players under 21 who have not moved on to junior hockey.

Pee-Wee Power

Since it began in 1960, the Quebec International Pee-Wee Hockey Tournament has seen almost 1,000 of its players go on to careers in the NHL. No wonder the event is billed as "the most important minor hockey tournament in the world."

The tournament takes place in Quebec City over 11 days in February and draws close to 200,000 fans every year. It often features 100 or more teams and over 2,000 players from as many as 16 different countries. NHL legends Guy Lafleur, Wayne Gretzky and Mario Lemieux all starred at the Quebec

MINOR HOCKEY CATEGORIES

Novice Under 9 (ages 7 and 8)
Goals: fun; reviewing basic skills; refining basic skills

Atom Under 11 (ages 9 and 10)
Goals: fun; refining basic skills; introduction to team tactics

Pee–wee Under 13 (ages 11 and 12)
Goals: fun; refining individual tactics; introduction to team play

Bantam Under 15 (ages 13 and 14)
Goals: fun; refining team play; introduction to team strategy

Midget Under 17 (ages 15 and 16)
Goals: fun; refining team play and strategy

tournament as young boys. More recent NHL stars who played there include Steven Stamkos, Johnny Gaudreau and Ryan Nugent-Hopkins. In 2016, a girls' team played at the tournament for the very first time.

JUNIOR ACHIEVEMENT

Junior is the highest level of youth hockey. It is generally for players between the ages of 16 and 20. Players don't receive a salary, so junior hockey is considered by most people to be amateur hockey. Players in the minor leagues do receive a full salary. They are usually 21 years of age or older, but still need more training to reach the NHL.

In the Western Hockey League, players can be drafted after their final year of bantam hockey and sometimes start in

junior hockey when they're as young as 15. In the Ontario Hockey League and in Quebec, a player has to be given "Exceptional Status" to play junior hockey at that age. So far, only five players have been granted this status. The first three have all gone on to become big stars in the NHL. They are John Tavares, Aaron Ekblad and Connor McDavid.

GATEWAY TO THE NHL

Every summer since 1963, a short time after the Stanley Cup has been won, the NHL holds its annual draft. This is where the dreams of a pro hockey career become more of a reality for the many young players developing their skills in junior hockey. From its beginning in 1963 until 1978, the draft was known as the Amateur Draft. That was because only

Quebec's Les Etoiles and their coach, four-time Olympic gold medallist Caroline Ouellette, preparing for the famous Quebec International Pee-Wee Hockey Tournament in Quebec City, 2016.

junior players, who had never played professional hockey before, were eligible for the draft. At the end of the 1978–79 season, the NHL took in four new teams from the World Hockey Association.

WHA teams were only allowed to keep a few of their players on their rosters when they entered the NHL. Many other former WHA players became eligible for the NHL draft in 1979. Since these players were already professionals, it didn't seem right to call it the Amateur Draft any more, so the name was changed to the NHL Entry Draft. A lot of people still call it the Entry Draft to this day, but the league has called it The NHL Draft since 2012.

The NHL Draft has become the gateway to the NHL for players from all around the world. From a low of just 11 players selected in 1965 to a high of 293 picks in 2000, more than 10,000 players have been drafted by NHL teams over the years . . . but not nearly that many have made it all the way to the big league. As the saying goes, "many are called, but few are chosen."

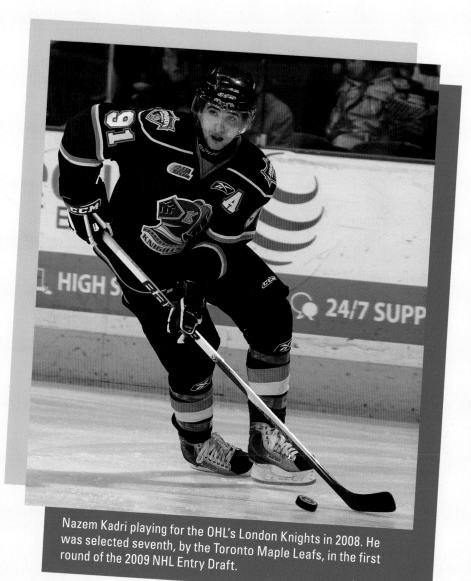

Nazem Kadri playing for the OHL's London Knights in 2008. He was selected seventh, by the Toronto Maple Leafs, in the first round of the 2009 NHL Entry Draft.

John Tavares pulls on his New York Islanders jersey after being picked first overall in the 2009 NHL Entry Draft.

DRAFT ORDER

Ever since 1969, the NHL has used the final standings as the order in which the teams get to pick in the draft. Picks used to be based entirely on the reverse order of the final standings. That meant the team with the league's worst record was always guaranteed to pick first.

Over the years, there were concerns that bad teams tried to do even worse to make sure they got the first draft pick. So ever since 1995, the NHL has used a special lottery to decide the order in

which teams will choose in the first round. These days, the 14 teams that miss the playoffs are all included in the draft lottery, and since 2016, the top three picks were all up for grabs.

However, the lottery is always set up so that the worst teams in the NHL have the best odds of getting the highest draft picks. That means the last-place team in the NHL is guaranteed no worse than the fourth draft pick.

For the 16 teams that do make the playoffs, their order of selection in the draft is determined by a combination of their points in the regular season and how far they go in the playoffs. The farther you go, the worse your pick. The team that wins the Stanley Cup picks last in the draft that year. After the first round, the order for the rest of the draft is determined only by the standings and playoff order. The draft lottery doesn't affect rounds two through seven.

AGE RANGE

For the first NHL draft in 1963, players were eligible to be selected if they turned 17 between August 1, 1963, and July 1, 1964.

The minimum age was increased to 18 in 1965 and then to 20 in 1967. It went back down to 18 in 1974, but back up to 20 in 1975. It returned to 18 in 1980 and has remained there ever since.

Technically, a player can be drafted while he is still 17, as long as he reaches his 18th birthday before September 15th of that year. For example, Sidney Crosby was only 17 years old when Pittsburgh picked him first overall at the 2005 NHL Entry Draft. He celebrated his 18th birthday a few weeks later, on August 7. On the other hand, players like Alex Ovechkin (born September 17, 1985), John Tavares (September 20, 1990) and Auston Matthews (September 17, 1997) had to wait until they were almost 19 to be drafted because of their "late" birth dates.

ROUND AND ROUND

In 1979, the NHL decided to limit the number of rounds in the draft, to six. Since then, the number of rounds has changed from time to time, going up as high as nine rounds in some years. It's currently at seven rounds.

When it was called the Amateur Draft there was no limit on the number of rounds. The draft just kept going on and on as long as even one team still wanted to pick more players. The 1974 Amateur Draft stretched on for a record 25 rounds!

IN THE CREASE

Garry Monahan was just 16 years and seven months old when he was picked in the first NHL draft in 1963, by the Montreal Canadiens.

NHL FIRSTS AND RECORDS

FIRST GOAL IN NHL HISTORY

The first NHL games were played on December 19, 1917. The Montreal Wanderers hosted the Toronto Arenas and beat them 10–9. The Montreal Canadiens were in Ottawa and beat the Senators 7–4. The Canadiens game in Ottawa was scheduled to start at 8:30 that night but was delayed for about 15 minutes. The Wanderers and Arenas faced off in Montreal at 8:15, officially making it the NHL's first game. Dave Ritchie of the Wanderers scored just one minute into the first period in the game against Toronto, giving him the honour of scoring the first goal in NHL history.

Most Goals
One game: 7 — Joe Malone, Quebec Bulldogs; January 31, 1920
One season: 92 — Wayne Gretzky, Edmonton Oilers; 1981–82 (80 games)
In a career: 894 — Wayne Gretzky, 20 seasons (1487 games)

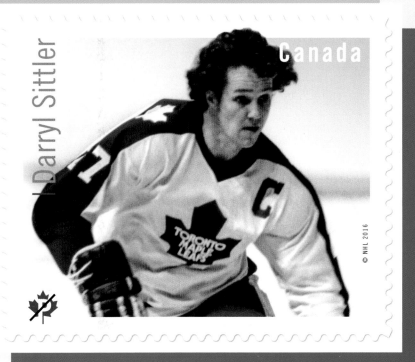

Darryl Sittler holds the record for most points in one game. He was included in Canada Post's Great Canadian Forwards series, issued in 2016.

Most Assists

One game: 7 — Billy Taylor,
Detroit Red Wings; March 16, 1947
7 — Wayne Gretzky, Edmonton Oilers;
three times
One season: 163 — Wayne Gretzky,
Edmonton Oilers; 1985–86 (80 games)
In a career: 1963 — Wayne Gretzky,
20 seasons (1487 games)

Most Points

One game: 10* — Darryl Sittler,
Toronto Maple Leafs; February 7, 1976
One season: 215† — Wayne Gretzky,
Edmonton Oilers; 1985–86 (80 games)
In a career: 2857 — Wayne Gretzky,
20 seasons (1487 games)

* Sittler had six goals and four assists

† Gretzky had 52 goals and 163 assists

On March 23, 1952, Bill Mosienko of the Chicago Blackhawks scored on New York Rangers goalie Lorne Anderson three times in 21 seconds — still the fastest hat trick in NHL history.

FIRST HAT TRICK

When a player scores three goals in a game, fans will often throw hats onto the ice. That's because scoring three goals in a game is known as a hat trick. In fact, doing three of almost anything in sports these days is often referred to as a hat trick. The term comes from cricket, but it's best known as a hockey term.

The first hat trick in NHL history came on the league's first night. In fact, there were a bunch of them! Harry Hyland had five goals for the Wanderers in their 10–9 win over Toronto; Joe Malone scored five for the Canadiens in their 7–4 win over Ottawa; Reg Noble scored four goals for Toronto that night and Cy Denneny scored three for the Senators.

YOUNG GUNS

When the Edmonton Oilers made Connor McDavid their captain at the start of his second season, in 2016–17, he became the youngest captain in NHL history. McDavid was just 19 years and 266 days old. He was 20 days younger than the former record holder, Gabriel Landeskog,

who was 19 years, 286 days old when Colorado gave him the "C" in 2012–13. Sidney Crosby was 19 years, 297 days old when he became captain of the Penguins in 2007–08.

FIRST OVERTIME GAME

From its first season in 1917–18 through 1920–21, every tie game in the NHL that went into overtime was played until there was a winner, no matter how long it took. The first NHL game to go into overtime was played on January 5, 1918. Joe Malone of the Canadiens scored the winner to give Montreal a 6–5 victory over the Ottawa Senators.

FIRST TIE GAME

Before the 1921–22 season, the NHL changed its rules about overtime. The league decided that if a game remained tied after one complete overtime period (20 minutes) it would end in a tie. On February 11, 1922, the Ottawa Senators and the Toronto St. Patricks played the NHL's first tie game with a score of 4–4.

IN THE CREASE

In his debut game on October 12, 2016, Auston Matthews scored four goals — the first to do so since the very first NHL game was played.

FIRST SHOOTOUT

The NHL got rid of overtime in the regular season on November 21, 1942. It wouldn't return until the 1983–84 season. Since then, overtime has been a five-minute, sudden-death period. Since the 2015–16 season, it's been played with three skaters and a goalie on the ice for each team. In 2005–06, the NHL introduced the shootout to decide a winner for games that are still tied after overtime. (Shootouts had already been used for several years in international hockey and the minor leagues.) Martin Havlat of the Ottawa Senators became the first player to score a shootout goal, on the very first night of the 2005–06 season.

Milestone Moments

First 50-goal season: Maurice Richard, Montreal Canadiens; 1944–45 (50-game season)

First to score more than 50 goals in one season: Bobby Hull, Chicago Blackhawks; 1965–66 (54 goals in a 70-game season)

First to score 500 career goals: Maurice Richard, Montreal Canadiens; October 19, 1957

First 100-point season: Phil Esposito, Boston Bruins; 1968–69 (126 points)

First defenceman to score 1000 career points: Denis Potvin, New York Islanders; April 4, 1987

Maurice "Rocket" Richard was the first to score 50 goals in a season and the first to reach 500 career goals.

First to score 1000 career points:
Gordie Howe, Detroit Red Wings;
November 27, 1960

First to play 1000 games: Gordie Howe,
Detroit Red Wings; November 26, 1961

Goalie Milestones

Most wins in one season: 48 — Martin
Brodeur, New Jersey Devils; 2006–07,
48 — Braden Holtby, Washington
Capitals; 2015–16

First to 300 career wins: Turk Broda,
Toronto Maple Leafs; December 20, 1950

First to 400 career wins: Terry
Sawchuk, Toronto Maple Leafs;
February 4, 1965

First to 500 career wins: Patrick Roy,
Colorado Avalanche; December 26, 2001

Most Career Wins: 691— Martin
Brodeur, New Jersey Devils,
St. Louis Blues

First to 100 shutouts: Terry Sawchuk,
Toronto Maple Leafs; March 4, 1967

Most career shutouts: 125 — Martin
Brodeur, New Jersey Devils, St, Louis Blues

MOST SHUTOUTS IN ONE SEASON

George Hainsworth set an NHL record that
is likely never to be broken when he posted
22 shutouts for the Montreal Canadiens
during the 1928–29 season. Making his
record even more remarkable, that NHL
season was just 44 games long. Hainsworth
allowed 43 goals in those 44 games with
his goals-against average of 0.92, setting
another record that should last forever.

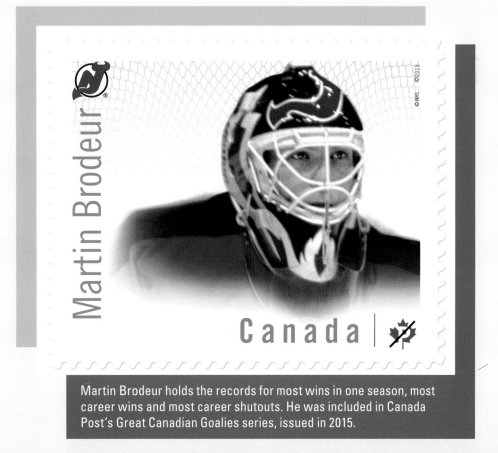

Martin Brodeur holds the records for most wins in one season, most career wins and most career shutouts. He was included in Canada Post's Great Canadian Goalies series, issued in 2015.

Team Records

Most wins, one season:
62 — Detroit Red Wings, 1995–96
(62–13–7 in 82 games)
60 — Montreal Canadiens, 1976–77
(60–8–12 in 80 games)
59 — Montreal Canadiens, 1977–78
(59–10–11 in 80 games)

Most points, one season:
132 — Montreal Canadiens, 1976–77
(60–8–12 in 80 games)
131 — Detroit Red Wings, 1995–96
(62–13–7 in 82 games)
129 — Montreal Canadiens, 1977–78
(59–10–11 in 80 games)

Most losses, one season:
71 — San Jose Sharks, 1992–93
(11–71–2 in 84 games)
70 — Ottawa Senators, 1992–93
(10–70–4 in 80 games)
67 — Washington Capitals, 1974–75
(8–67–5 in 80 games)

STREAKS

The NHL records for the longest winning streak and the longest losing streak are both 17 games. The Pittsburgh Penguins won 17 in a row from March 9 to April 10, 1993. As for losing, two teams share that record. The Washington Capitals lost 17 in a row from February 18 to March 26, 1975, while the San Jose Sharks lost 17 straight between January 4 and February 12, 1993.

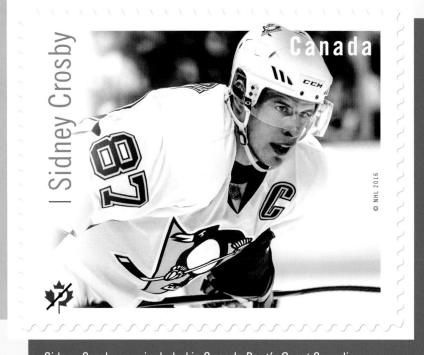

Sidney Crosby was included in Canada Post's Great Canadian Forwards series, issued in 2016 — the only active player in the set.

FIRST OUTDOOR NHL GAME

The NHL's Winter Classic has become a New Year's tradition, with teams facing off in football stadiums or baseball parks. But the NHL's first outdoor game was anything but wintery. It was more like a duel in the desert.

On September 27, 1991, the New York Rangers met the Los Angeles Kings for a pre-season exhibition game in Las Vegas. The rink was set up in a parking lot outside the famous Caesars Palace casino and the temperatures hit 29°C (84°F). Wayne Gretzky led the Kings to a 5–2 victory. "We kept looking at each other," Gretzky remembered, "and couldn't believe we were playing hockey in 80-degree weather. But it was real nice."

FIRST REGULAR-SEASON OUTDOOR GAME

On November 22, 2003, the Edmonton Oilers hosted the Montreal Canadiens in an outdoor game at Commonwealth Stadium. A crowd of 57,167 braved freezing temperatures (−18°C / 0°F) but saw the hometown team lose the game 4–3.

The first Winter Classic was played on January 1, 2008, at Ralph Wilson Stadium in Buffalo, New York. In a light snowfall, Sidney Crosby's shootout goal gave the Pittsburgh Penguins a 2–1 win over the Sabres.

BIGGEST GAME EVER?

The largest crowd in NHL history attended the 2014 Winter Classic between the Detroit Red Wings and the Toronto Maple Leafs. It was played at the University of Michigan football stadium — known as "The Big House" — in Ann Arbor, Michigan. A total of 105,491 tickets were sold for that game. That should have set an all-time hockey record, but the people at Guinness World Records disagree. Guinness only counts the number of tickets scanned upon entry on the day of the game. On game day, the cold, snowy weather meant many people were arriving late and the ticket takers stopped scanning tickets! So, while the NHL counts the attendance as 105,491, the official all-time hockey attendance record stands at 104,173, for a different game at the same stadium. That game was between the University of Michigan and their rivals from Michigan State on December 11, 2010. The University of Michigan claims that 113,411 tickets were actually sold for that game . . . of which Guinness World Records says 104,173 were scanned.

WOMEN IN HOCKEY

Isobel Stanley (the player in white) was the star player in Ottawa in the early 1890s. She was the daughter of Lord Stanley, who donated the Stanley Cup.

Girls and women have been playing hockey in Canada since the late 1880s. In those early days, games were often played without any spectators in case anything "unladylike" should occur. Women's hockey gained popularity during World War I and was played competitively in Canada and the United States during the 1920s. On March 22, 1929, 12,000 people filled the Montreal Forum for a charity hockey game in which the Ontario champion Patterson Pats of Toronto defeated the Quebec champion Northern Electrics from Verdun, 2–0. The women's game continued to thrive with regular provincial and national championships throughout the 1930s.

PRESTON LADIES ARE CHAMPIONS

Even in the midst of the Great Depression, the Preston Rivulettes attracted large crowds of appreciative fans, who were always treated to a show of fast, exciting hockey.

THE RIVULETTES

If the tale is true, the greatest team in the history of women's hockey was formed on a dare back in 1930. As the story goes, the members of the Preston Rivulettes girls' softball team were holding a meeting at the local arena. They were trying to decide what to do once the softball season ended. Someone suggested they form a hockey team. Someone else laughed and dared them to do it . . . so they did.

That winter, the Rivulettes joined the Ladies Ontario Hockey Association. Playing against teams from Toronto, Kitchener, Stratford, London, Hamilton, Guelph and Port Dover, the Rivulettes proved to be the best. Led by their star player, Hilda Ranscombe, they won the Ontario championship that season and went on to win it 10 years in a row. They were champions of Canada six times. In all, it's believed that the Preston team played about 350 games during those 10 years. They won all but five of them, suffering only two losses and three ties.

The Rivulettes were invited to play in Europe in 1939, but the tour was cancelled after the start of World War II. The war hurt the team even worse before the start of 1940–41 season. Gasoline rationing meant they could no longer meet their travel commitments, so the Rivulettes had to fold.

BOBBIE WAS THE BEST

In 1932, Bobbie Rosenfeld was voted the best women's hockey player in Ontario. Most sources say Rosenfeld led the Patterson Pats to the Ontario Women's Hockey Championship in 1927 and 1929, but in fact they won in 1926 and 1929 (they lost in the finals in 1927). Rosenfeld was also voted Canada's Female Athlete of the Half-Century in 1950. She starred in many sports, including basketball, softball, tennis and golf. In 1928, she won gold and silver medals as a sprinter at the Summer Olympics.

NO GIRLS ALLOWED

After lean times during World War II, hockey for girls and women had pretty much disappeared by the 1950s. But in the fall of 1955, eight-year-old Abby Hoffman decided that she wanted to play on an organized team. She'd been playing since she was three and liked to play with her older brother. So that fall she cut her hair short, called herself Ab and earned a spot on the Little St. Catharines Tee Pees in the Toronto Hockey League. Ab played defence well enough to earn a spot in a charity all-star game, but she had to show her birth certificate to play. Organizers were stunned to discover that she was a girl. The story made headlines in newspapers and magazines all across North America.

Hoffman was allowed to finish the season with her team, but she was barred from playing with boys after that. Even though 90 girls showed up at a practice the following winter, attempts to organize a girls' division in the Toronto Hockey League were rejected by the men who ran it.

Abby Hoffman later helped to organize a girls' hockey team at her Toronto high school, but focused more on track and field and swimming. She competed in track and field at the Summer Olympics in 1964, 1968, 1972 and 1976. Later, she would become the first woman elected to the executive of the Canadian Olympic Committee and the first woman to run Sport Canada.

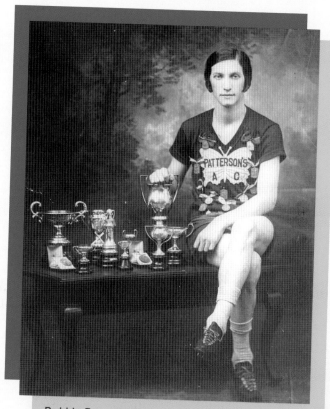

Bobbie Rosenfeld stopped competing in 1933, but dedicated the rest of her life to women's sports. She coached, ran several hockey and softball organizations and was a sports journalist for the *Globe and Mail* for 20 years.

THE GAME BOUNCES BACK

Women's hockey made a comeback in the 1960s. A big step came in 1967, when the Dominion Ladies Hockey Tournament was held in Brampton, Ontario. The tournament featured 22 teams from all across the province, with players ranging in age from nine to 50.

More and more Canadian provinces created teams and leagues for girls and women in the 1970s, as did some high schools and universities in the United States. Countries like Finland, Japan, Sweden, China, Korea, Norway, Germany and Switzerland soon followed.

By 1982, women's hockey had become popular enough in Canada to hold the first national championship tournament since the 1930s. Abby Hoffman was one of the organizers, and from 1982 until 2008, the top women's teams in

Canada competed for the Abby Hoffman Cup. Support for the women's game has continued to grow since the 1980s. According to Hockey Canada, there were just over 8,000 female hockey players registered to play across the country during the winter of 1990–91. By 2008–09, the number had risen to more than 80,000 and it keeps on growing!

SHIRLEY CAMERON AND THE EDMONTON CHIMOS

In 1973, the Edmonton Chimos were born. One of the founding members of the team was Shirley Cameron. She would become the first superstar of modern women's hockey.

Cameron and the Chimos dominated women's hockey in Alberta. They won every provincial championship but one

Abby Hoffman and teammates, taken in 1957. Team captain Jim Halliday said of Abby "He — she — is just one of the gang. Good hockey player, too. I hope we don't lose him — her, I mean."

between 1982 to 1997. They also won the Canadian championship in 1984, 1985 and 1992. Cameron coached the team to another title in 1997. The Chimos remained active in women's hockey through the 2010–11 season. In 2011–12, the Chimos combined with the Strathmore Rockies (later becoming the Calgary Inferno) to become Team Alberta in the Canadian Women's Hockey League.

MANON MAKES HER MARK

Manon Rheaume won World Championships as a goalie with the Canadian National Women's Team in 1992 and 1994 and an Olympic silver medal in 1998, but she's best known for her milestones in men's hockey. On November 26, 1991, she became the first woman to play major junior hockey in Canada as a member of the Trois-Rivieres Draveurs in the Quebec Major Junior Hockey League. On September 23, 1992, Rheaume became the first woman to play in the NHL. A scout had noticed Rheaume's goaltending abilities and sent a video of a Trois-Rivieres game to Phil Esposito, who was starting the Tampa Bay Lightning expansion team. The scout did not say anything about the goalie being female. Esposito was surprised, but decided to give her a shot. She saw action for one period with the Tampa Bay Lightning against the St. Louis Blues and in a pre-season game against the Boston Bruins in 1993.

Today, Manon Rheaume helps run a girls' hockey program in Detroit, Michigan, and has started a scholarship foundation to help young women advance their athletic careers.

The Clarkson Cup was not actually handed out until 2009. There were disagreements between the artists of the cup and there were changes in the leagues. The Montreal Stars won the first championship, beating the Minnesota Whitecaps 3–1 in the final.

THE CLARKSON CUP

When the NHL season was cancelled by a lockout in 2004–05, many people still hoped to see the Stanley Cup awarded somehow. Adrienne Clarkson, the governor general of Canada, suggested awarding the Stanley Cup to the best team in women's hockey. No one really went for that idea, but it was suggested that, since Lord Stanley had been governor general when he donated the cup for men's hockey, that Madame Clarkson should donate a brand new trophy for women's hockey. So she did.

The Clarkson Cup is made of silver. It's not nearly as big as the Stanley Cup, but includes the Clarkson coat of arms and symbols of Inuit art. In 2006, the trophy was presented for the first time, as an honorary award to the Canadian National Women's Team who had won the gold medal at that year's Winter Olympics. Teams from the Canadian Women's Hockey League have played for the Clarkson Cup since 2009.

WOMEN'S LEAGUES TODAY

For many female hockey players around the world, the highest level of hockey they can reach is playing university hockey in the United States. A lot of the women's players you see representing their countries at the Olympics or the World Championship have played for American universities. But after a player graduates, it's often tough for her to find a good league to play in.

Many different leagues for women have come and gone over the years. Today, the Canadian Women's Hockey League (CWHL) is the top women's league in the country. It currently has five teams: les Canadiennes de Montreal, the Toronto Furies, the Brampton Thunder, the Calgary Inferno and the Boston Blades. The National Women's Hockey League (NWHL) is the top

American league for women. Its four teams are the Boston Pride, the Buffalo Beauts, the Connecticut Whale and the New York Riveters. The champions of the NWHL receive the Isobel Cup — named after Isobel Stanley, whose father donated the Stanley Cup.

Women playing in these two leagues have to be very dedicated to their sport. The CWHL covers most of the players' expenses, but doesn't pay salaries. The NWHL does pay its players, but the salaries are very small. That means everyone playing in these leagues has to have an off-ice job too, and has to juggle a work career and a playing career.

HALL OF FAME FIRSTS

Bobbie Rosenfeld was one of the first people honoured when Canada's Sports Hall of Fame opened in 1955, but for her track and field achievements. It would take more than 50 years for a woman to be elected to Canada's Sports Hall of Fame as a hockey player. Today, the Hockey Hall of Fame, the U.S. Hockey Hall of Fame and the International

Ice Hockey Federation Hall of Fame all honour female members, but these four were the first.

Cassie Campbell

In 2007 Cassie Campbell became the first women's hockey player elected to Canada's Sports Hall of Fame. Campbell spent 12 years with Canada's National Women's Team, from 1994 to 2006. She became captain of the team in 2001 and was the first hockey player in Canadian history — male or female — to captain a team to two Olympic gold medals, with victories in 2002 and 2006. She also won six World Championship gold medals in her career, including two as captain. She has covered men's and women's hockey on television since 2006.

Angela James

Angela James grew up playing hockey with boys in her hometown of Toronto. In 1980, when she was just 15, she began playing with much older women in the Ontario Women's Hockey Association. She went on to win eight scoring titles and six Most Valuable Player awards. In 1990, James led Team Canada with 11

IN THE CREASE

Sarah and Amy Potomak of Aldergrove, British Columbia, became the first sisters to suit up together for the Canadian women's hockey team during a two-game series against the United States near the end of December 2016. What a nice Christmas present for their family!

goals in five games at the first Women's World Championship.

In 2010, James was one of the first two women elected to the Hockey Hall of Fame. She'd been elected to Canada's Sports Hall of Fame in 2009 and to the International Ice Hockey Federation Hall of Fame in 2008.

Cammi Granato

American Cammi Granato was elected to both the International Ice Hockey Federation Hall of Fame in 2008 and to the Hockey Hall of Fame in 2010 along with Angela James. She was also elected to the U.S. Hockey Hall of Fame in 2008.

Granato was one of six children in her family, including her brother Tony, who grew up to play in the NHL. She played on boys' hockey teams from age 5 to 16, and went on to star in women's hockey at Providence College in the United States and Concordia University in Canada. Granato was a member of the U.S. Women's National team from 1990 to 2005. She captained the American team to an Olympic gold medal in 1998.

Cassie Campbell celebrates her 2003 National Women's Hockey League championship with her team, Calgary Oval X-Treme

Geraldine Heaney

Geraldine Heaney was elected to the International Ice Hockey Federation Hall of Fame, along with James and Granato, in 2008. She was elected to the Hockey Hall of Fame in 2013 and to Canada's Sports Hall of Fame in 2014. Heaney began playing with the Toronto Aeros in the Ontario Women's Hockey Association when she was only 13 years old. She went on to play 18 seasons with the Aeros, winning six provincial championships. Heaney won the Women's World Championship seven times with Team Canada between 1990 and 2001, and an Olympic gold medal in 2002.

Other Honoured Players

- **Hockey Hall of Fame:**
  Angela Ruggiero (2015)
- **U.S. Hockey Hall of Fame:**
  Karen Bye (2014)
  Cindy Curley (2013)
  Angela Ruggiero (2015)
- **IIHF Hall of Fame:**
  Riika Nieminen-Valila (2010)
  Karen Bye (2011)
  Danielle Goyette (2013)
  Angela Ruggiero (2017)
  Maria Rooth (2015)
- **Canada's Sports Hall of Fame:**
  Hilda Ranscombe (2015)

THE BEST EVER?

When Hayley Wickenheiser was young, people used to tell her that girls didn't play hockey. She grew up to become the best female hockey player in the world. She might just be the best of all time.

In 1998 and 1999, she attended rookie training camp with the Philadelphia Flyers. In 2003, she signed to play with a men's team, HC Salamat, in Finland, and on February 1, 2003, she became the first woman to score a goal in men's professional hockey. In 2007, Wickenheiser became the first women's hockey player to receive the Bobbie Rosenfeld Award as Canada's Female Athlete of the Year.

Wickenheiser started skating in her hometown of Shaunavon, Saskatchewan, when she was three or four years old. She began playing hockey when she was five. Mostly, she had to play on boys' teams. Usually, she was the best player on those teams. In 1991, when she was 12, Wickenheiser played for Team Alberta the first time women's hockey was played at the Canada Winter Games. Many of the other girls in the tournament were 17, but Wickenheiser scored the winning goal and was named the MVP in the gold medal game.

By the time she was 15, Wickenheiser earned a spot on the Canadian National Women's Team for the 1994 Women's World Championship. She remained with the team until she was 38 years old, and announced her retirement on January 13, 2017. Wickenheiser played in 13 World Championships (she missed 2001 and 2015 due to injuries), winning seven gold medals and six silvers. She also played at the Winter Olympics five times, winning four golds and one silver and being named tournament MVP in 2002 and 2006. In all, Hayley Wickenheiser represented Canada in 276 international games, scoring 168 goals and 211 assists for 379 points.

Hayley Wickenheiser of Team Canada after a gold-medal performance at the 2012 Women's World Championships.

INTERNATIONAL HIGHLIGHTS

THE INTERNATIONAL ICE HOCKEY FEDERATION

Outside of Canada and the United States, hockey in the 1890s was most popular in Great Britain. By 1903, there was a small hockey league there.

On May 15, 1908, Great Britain was one of the first five founding members when the International Ice Hockey Federation (IIHF) was formed in Paris. France was also a founding member. The others were Switzerland, Belgium and Bohemia (which later became Czechoslovakia, and is now the Czech Republic). Until 1954, the IIHF was known by the French name, *Ligue Internationale de Hockey sur Glace*.

In 1909, Germany became the sixth member. The first games organized by this new hockey group were played in Berlin that November. The first European Championship was held in 1910. It was won by Great Britain — though their team boasted many Canadian players. During the 1920s and 1930s, the European Championship became part of the Olympics and World Championship.

Today, the objectives of the IIHF are to govern, develop and promote hockey throughout the world, to control international hockey and to promote

Tsewang Chuskit on a breakaway in the India vs. Philippines game during the 2017 IIHF Ice Hockey Women's Challenge Cup of Asia on March 9, 2017.

friendly relations between hockey playing countries. As of 2016, the IIHF has 77 members in Europe, North America, South American, Asia, Australia and Africa. There are four different levels of Men's World Championships. The IIHF is also responsible for organizing the Women's World Championship and the World Under-20 Championship (more commonly known as the World Junior Hockey Championship) as well as the World Under-18 Championships for men and for women.

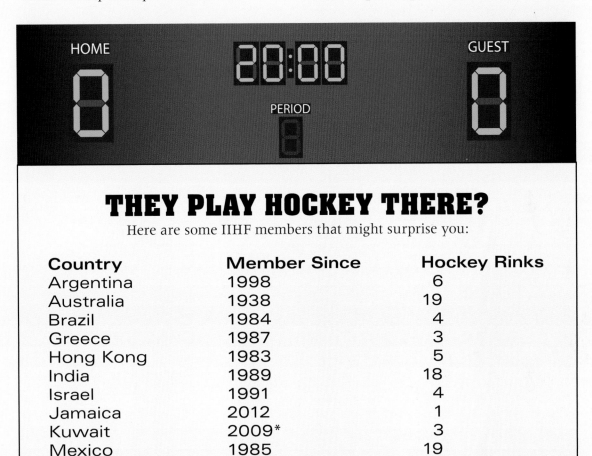

THEY PLAY HOCKEY THERE?

Here are some IIHF members that might surprise you:

Country	Member Since	Hockey Rinks
Argentina	1998	6
Australia	1938	19
Brazil	1984	4
Greece	1987	3
Hong Kong	1983	5
India	1989	18
Israel	1991	4
Jamaica	2012	1
Kuwait	2009*	3
Mexico	1985	19
Mongolia	1999	21
Morocco	2010	2
New Zealand	1977	11
Qatar	2012	3
Portugal	1999	1
South Africa	1937	8
Spain	1923	17
Thailand	1989	13
Turkey	1991	29
United Arab Emirates	2001	9

*Kuwait was previously a member from 1985 to 1992

OLYMPIC HOCKEY

Hockey was first played at the Olympics in 1920. There were no separate Winter Olympic Games, so hockey was part of a spring sports festival before the 1920 Summer Games in Antwerp, Belgium. Canada was represented by the Winnipeg Falcons, who had won the Allan Cup as the top amateur team in the country. The Falcons brought home Canada's first Olympic hockey gold medal! The first

Winter Olympics were held in Chamonix, France, in 1924, and hockey has been played at the Winter Olympics ever since.

For years, hockey at the Olympics was only for amateur players. A few professionals were allowed to play for the first time at the 1988 Winter Olympics in Calgary. Full participation by NHL players began in 1998 at the Winter Games in Nagano, Japan. Women's hockey also made its Olympic debut in 1998.

The Winnipeg Falcons' gold-medal Olympic Team in 1920. At that time hockey and figure skating were part of the Summer Olympic Games.

WORLD CHAMPIONSHIPS

The hockey tournament played at the Olympics in 1920 is often considered to be the first World Championship, too. In fact, all the Olympic tournaments played through 1972 also doubled as World Championship events. But the first true World Championship was held in 1930.

Ten European countries participated in Championship games, along with a team from Japan and one from Canada. Canada's team was a Toronto-based amateur club representing the CCM sporting goods company. They were already touring Europe when the tournament was scheduled. Since Canada was already known as a hockey powerhouse, the Toronto team was given a free pass directly into the finals! Germany proved to be the best of the rest, but Canada beat the Germans 6–1 in the championship game. Between 1930 and 1961, Canada won the World Championship 16 times in 25 tournaments . . . but things got a lot tougher after that.

RISE OF THE RUSSIANS

Hockey was first introduced to Russia in 1932. However, the game was not nearly as popular at first as the Russian winter sport of bandy.

Russia didn't have its own hockey league until 1946. Then, a big boost to the game came in 1948, when the LTC Prague team from Czechoslovakia visited Moscow. Many players on that Czech team had won silver medals in hockey at the 1948 Olympics. People thought they'd beat the Russians easily, but the Moscow Selects managed a win and a tie during the three-game series. The Russians worked hard at hockey after that. In 1954, Russia made its first appearance at the World Championship. They stunned Canada's team with a 7–2 victory in the final game, winning the gold medal. Two years later, Russia won the gold medal at the Olympics.

During this era, Russia was part of the Soviet Union (officially, the Union of Soviet Socialist Republics or USSR) where nobody was paid to play hockey. Most players on the Soviet national team were soldiers, but instead of training for military service, they trained to play hockey all year long.

From 1954 until the breakup of the Soviet Union in 1991, the USSR dominated international hockey. The Soviets won seven golds, a silver and a bronze at nine Olympic tournaments. They won the World Championships every year from 1963 to 1971. They added eleven more golds, three silvers and three bronze at World events through 1991.

International hockey has been much more even since 1992. Russia has still produced many great players, and they have won their share of medals, but the competition with Canada, the United States, Sweden, Finland, the Czech Republic and Slovakia has been more balanced — although Canada has begun to dominate again in recent years!

HOME

PERIOD

GUEST

OLYMPIC RESULTS
MEN'S

Year	Gold	Silver	Bronze	Host Country
1920	Canada	USA	Czechoslovakia	Belgium
1924	Canada	USA	Great Britain	France
1928	Canada	Sweden	Switzerland	Switzerland
1932	Canada	USA	Germany	USA
1936	Great Britain	Canada	USA	Germany
1948	Canada	Czechoslovakia	Switzerland	Switzerland
1952	Canada	USA	Sweden	Norway
1956	USSR	USA	Canada	Italy
1960	USA	Canada	USSR	USA
1964	USSR	Sweden	Czechoslovakia	Austria
1968	USSR	Czechoslovakia	Canada	France
1972	USSR	USA	Czechoslovakia	Japan
1976	USSR	Czechoslovakia	West Germany	Austria
1980	USA	USSR	Sweden	USA
1984	USSR	Czechoslovakia	Sweden	Yugoslavia
1988	USSR	Finland	Sweden	Canada
1992	Unified Team	Canada	Czechoslovakia	France
1994	Sweden	Canada	Finland	Norway
1998	Czech Republic	Russia	Finland	Japan
2002	Canada	USA	Russia	USA
2006	Sweden	Finland	Czech Republic	Italy
2010	Canada	USA	Finland	Canada
2014	Canada	Sweden	Finland	Russia

WOMEN'S

Year	Gold	Silver	Bronze	Host Country
1998	USA	Canada	Finland	Japan
2002	Canada	USA	Sweden	USA
2006	Canada	Sweden	USA	Italy
2010	Canada	USA	Finland	Canada
2014	Canada	USA	Switzerland	Russia

CHAMONIX M.-BLANC
TOUS LES SPORTS D'HIVER

The 1930 World Ice Hockey Championships were supposed to take place in Chamonix, France, but warm winter weather melted the ice. The officials moved the tournament to Berlin, Germany, where the Sportpalast rink had the technology to create artificially cooled ice.

CZECHS AND SWEDES

Around 1905, a Canadian student named John "Ruck" Anderson was studying violin in Prague, Bohemia. He introduced the local bandy players to hockey. By 1908, they had formed some hockey teams. Bohemia attended an unofficial IIHF tournament in 1909, and they won the European Championship in 1911 and 1914. After World War I, Bohemia became Czechoslovakia. In the 1940s, Czechoslovakia became a world hockey power and remained so for more than 40 years. In 1993, the country split into the Czech Republic and Slovakia. Both nations continue to produce world-class hockey players.

In Sweden, it was an American named Raoul Le Mat who introduced the country's bandy players to hockey in 1919. In 1920, Sweden sent a hockey team to the Olympics, and in 1921 they won the European Championship. Players from Sweden were some of the first Europeans to become stars in the NHL in the 1970s. Since the 1990s, Swedish teams have enjoyed great international success.

AMERICAN HISTORY

When hockey was becoming popular in Canada in the late 1800s, many Americans living in colder northern states played a similar game called ice polo. After Canadian teams began to visit the United States in the 1890s, American teams started to take hockey more seriously. It didn't take long for hockey to become much more popular than ice polo.

The United States formed the world's first professional hockey leagues in the early 1900s and in the early days of international hockey, American teams were almost always second-best, behind Canada. However, their gold medal victory ahead of Canada and the USSR on home ice at Squaw Valley, California, in 1960 was seen as a pretty big upset. Their Olympic victory at Lake Placid, New York, in 1980 was such a surprise it has been called the "Miracle on Ice."

THE WOMEN'S WORLD CHAMPIONSHIPS

The first Women's World Championship was held in Toronto in 1987, but the International Ice Hockey Federation did not recognize it as an official tournament. Even so, teams from Canada, the United States, Sweden, Switzerland, Japan and Holland took part. There was also a team representing the province of Ontario.

Three years later, the first official Women's World Championship was held in Ottawa. The Canadian team — which won the gold medal — wore pink uniforms instead of Canada's traditional red, which many people found controversial. Tournaments were played in 1992, 1994 and 1997, but ever since 1997, there has been a Women's World Championship scheduled every year, except for the Olympic years. Canada

In the 1890s, ice polo was far more popular than hockey in the United States.

Angela James scored 22 goals and 12 assists in 20 games over four Women's World Championships, including 11 goals in 5 games in the first IIHF World Women's Championships, held in Ottawa, Ontario, in 1990.

and the United States have dominated the Women's World Championships with the two countries winning the gold and silver medals at every single tournament.

THE WORLD JUNIORS

It's officially known as the World Under-20 Championship, but most Canadians know it as the World Junior Hockey Championship. It's a holiday tradition for many Canadian hockey fans in late December and early January. Millions watch the tournament on TV every year.

Three unofficial tournaments were held before the event truly got under way in the winter of 1976–77. The Soviets won all three of these, and the first four real ones as well. Sweden won the event in 1981.

In these early days, Canada didn't send a national team to the tournament as it does today. Usually, the team that won

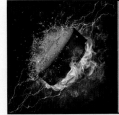

World Players
Like the Olympics, the World Championship used to be only for amateur players. But since 1977, players with NHL teams that have missed the playoffs or been eliminated early have been able to play at the World Championship.

the Memorial Cup as Canada's national junior champion competed.

Finally, in 1981–82, the idea of a national junior team was born. The result was Canada's first World Junior gold. After winning again in 1985, 1988, 1990 and 1991, Canada won five straight tournaments from 1993 through 1997. Canada won four silvers and two bronze medals from 1999 to 2004 but didn't win gold again until 2005. Many people consider that year's team to be Canada's best ever at the tournament. The team featured future NHL stars Dion Phaneuf and Shea Weber on defence as well as forwards Jeff Carter, Ryan Getzlaf, Corey Perry, Patrice Bergeron . . . and a 17-year-old kid named Sidney Crosby. That victory in 2005 kicked off another run of five straight gold medals for Canada.

SLEDGE HOCKEY

One of the most popular winter sports for athletes with physical disabilities is an adaptation of traditional ice hockey. Sledge hockey was invented in 1961 by three wheelchair athletes on a frozen lake in Stockholm, Sweden. It's played on specially designed sleds that have skate blades under their seats. Players sit on the sleds, holding a stick in each hand, and use their sticks to pass, shoot and stickhandle the puck, as well as to manoeuvre their sleds. The game's rules are basically the same as hockey's, and the sport is popular in many of the countries around the world where hockey is played. Sledge hockey has been part of the Paralympic Winter Games since 1994. The first World Championship tournament was held in 1996.

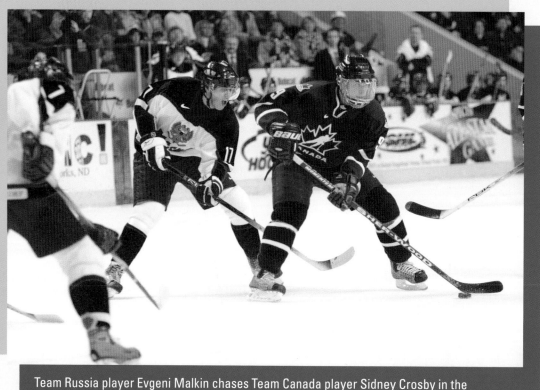

Team Russia player Evgeni Malkin chases Team Canada player Sidney Crosby in the 2005 World Junior Hockey Championship.

FAMOUS SERIES

THE 1972 SUMMIT SERIES

After dominating the early days of international hockey, things changed for Canada after the Soviet Union made its debut at the 1954 World Championship. Canadian amateurs could no longer keep up, and the Soviets soon took over. Still, most Canadians were sure the Soviets would be put in their place if they ever faced the best pros from the

Team Canada goalie Tony Esposito defends the net during game seven of the 1972 Summit Series on September 26, 1972.

NHL. But when Team Canada met the Soviets in an eight-game series in September of 1972, it was far tougher than anyone imagined.

Soviet players worked out all year. Canadian players didn't. The NHL players cut short their summer vacations for a three-week training camp, but nobody worked too hard. The series was going to be fun. Many people expected Canada to win all eight games. When the series began in Montreal on September 2, Team Canada scored 30 seconds after the opening faceoff. It was 2–0 Canada just a few minutes later. It was going to be an easy win . . . an easy series. However, when the game was over, the Soviets had rallied for a 7–3 victory. A nation was stunned.

Canada won the second game 4–1 in Toronto, but after a 4–4 tie in Winnipeg, the Soviets scored a 5–3 victory in Vancouver. Canadian players were shocked to hear fans booing them.

After a two-week break and some training games in Europe, Team Canada arrived in Moscow. It was more than just a hockey series now. It was our way of life against theirs: freedom and democracy in the western world against Communism and oppression in the east. But Team Canada lost the first game in Moscow 5–4. Now Canada had to win each of the last three games to save the series. It seemed they were on their way: they won 3–2 and 4–3, with Paul Henderson scoring the winning goal in both games. The showdown was on for game eight. Across Canada, people turned on television sets in homes, offices, schools . . . anywhere they could.

The game was tense. By the third period Canada was down 5–3. Things didn't look good. But Canada rallied for two goals. With time running out, Henderson scored with just 34 seconds remaining, to give Team Canada a 6–5 victory. Cheers could be heard across Canada. Nearly 50 years later, the Summit Series victory remains one of the greatest moments in Canadian history.

THE GREATEST GAME: MEN'S EDITION

During the 1975–76 NHL season, two teams from the Soviet Union came to North America for a special exhibition series. The match-ups were known as "Super Series '76."

The game between Moscow's Central Red Army and the Montreal Canadiens on New Year's Eve, December 31, 1975, was the one that everybody was looking forward to. The Canadiens were the greatest team in NHL history. The Red Army was the greatest team in Europe.

Canadian fans had seen how good the Soviet players were during the 1972 Summit Series. The Soviets used blazing speed and lots of short passes. They didn't shoot the puck a lot, but when they did, it was usually a good scoring chance. But the Canadiens were fast too . . . and they came out flying. They were out-skating the Red Army stars and because of their speed the Russians were making mistakes. The Canadiens jumped out to an early 2–0 lead and were up 3–1 midway through the second period. Montreal was playing a nearly perfect game. Only goalie Vladislav Tretiak was keeping the Red Army close. The shots on goal were 22–7 for the Canadiens when the second period ended, but

their lead had been cut to 3–2.

The Red Army tied the game early in the third period. The Canadiens played even harder. They fired 16 shots at Tretiak, but they couldn't beat him again. Montreal probably should have won the game, but somehow a 3–3 tie seemed fitting.

SUMMIT SERIES RESULTS

DATE	SCORE	LOCATION
September 2, 1972	USSR 7 Canada 3	Montreal
September 4, 1972	USSR 1 Canada 4	Toronto
September 6, 1972	USSR 4 Canada 4	Winnipeg
September 8, 1972	USSR 5 Canada 3	Vancouver
September 22, 1972	Canada 4 USSR 5	Moscow
September 24, 1972	Canada 3 USSR 2	Moscow
September 26, 1972	Canada 4 USSR 3	Moscow
September 28, 1972	Canada 6 USSR 5	Moscow

THE CANADA CUP

The Canada Cup was created in 1976. This new tournament allowed NHL players from Canada to compete against the best players from the United States, Sweden, Finland, Czechoslovakia and the Soviet Union.

Learning from their experience in 1972, Canadian players trained for the Canada Cup much more seriously than they had for the Summit Series. This time, they won the tournament pretty easily, although it took an overtime goal from Darryl Sittler to defeat Czechoslovakia in the final game. There are many people who believe the Team Canada roster from 1976 was the strongest team in hockey history. Of the 25 men on the roster, 17 eventually made it to the Hockey Hall of Fame.

The Canada Cup was held five times between 1976 and 1991. For many fans, the 1987 Canada Cup was the greatest tournament ever, featuring Wayne Gretzky and Mario Lemieux on Team Canada. The Final matched Team Canada against the Soviets in a three-game series where each game was more exciting than the one before. The Soviets won the first game 6–5 in overtime. Two nights later, Canada won 6–5 in double overtime. Gretzky had five assists and Lemieux scored three, including the winner. In the finale, Gretzky set up Lemieux again with 1:26 remaining as Team Canada wrapped up the series with another 6–5 win.

Mario Lemieux, Wayne Gretzky and Larry Murphy celebrate the game-winning goal scored against Team Soviet Union during game two of the 1987 Canada Cup Finals on September 13, 1987.

THE WORLD CUP

In 1996, the Canada Cup was reorganized as the World Cup of Hockey. The format expanded to include eight national teams and some of the games were played in European countries. Canada and the United States reached the best-of-three final, but after Canada won the first games, the United States won two straight to take the tournament. It would be eight years before another World Cup, and this time Canada came out on top.

The World Cup of Hockey would not resume again until 2016. Once again eight teams took part, but this time, there was a twist. In addition to Canada, the United States, Russia, Sweden, Finland and the Czech Republic, there was a Team Europe made up of players from eight different countries and a Team North America made up of young players from Canada and the United States who were all age 23 or under.

Brad Marchand scored the winning goal for Team Canada against Team Europe in the final game of the 2016 World Cup, and Sidney Crosby was named the most valuable player. Even so, many of the highlights of the tournament were provided by Team North America. Led by their captain, Connor McDavid, their top scorer Johnny Gaudreau, and newcomer Auston Matthews (who hadn't even played in the NHL yet!) this young team played a fast, exciting game and proved that the future of hockey is in good hands!

HOME   20:00   GUEST

PERIOD

CANADA CUP AND WORLD CUP RESULTS

Year	Champion	Finalist
1976	Canada	Czechoslovakia
1981	USSR	Canada
1984	Canada	Sweden
1987	Canada	USSR
1991	Canada	USA
1996	USA	Canada
2004	Canada	Finland
2016	Canada	Europe

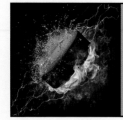
THE MIRACLE ON ICE

The 1980 Winter Olympics were held in Lake Placid, New York. Even on home ice, the Americans weren't expected to do very well. NHL all-star teams had trouble beating the powerful Soviet Union, so no one thought a U.S. team filled with college players had any chance. In fact, the Soviets beat Team USA 10–3 in an exhibition game shortly before the Olympics.

The Americans rallied to tie Sweden 2–2 in their first Olympic game. When they won their next four straight, people all across the United States who'd never paid much attention to hockey were suddenly caught up in this underdog story. Next up was a medal-round rematch with the Soviets. The Americans were outshot 39–16, and yet they pulled off a shocking 4–3 upset. Television broadcaster Al Michaels summed up the moment best as the game wound down. "Do you believe in miracles? . . . Yes!"

But the Miracle on Ice wouldn't truly be complete without a victory in the final game. When the Americans beat Finland 4–2, the gold medal was theirs.

A LONG TIME COMING

After a victory by the amateur Edmonton Mercurys at the 1952 Winter Games in Oslo, Norway, Canada would have to wait a long time for its next Olympic hockey gold. Many people expected Canada to win in 1998 when the NHL first shut down its season to allow players to take part at the Nagano Olympics, but instead, they finished fourth. It didn't look much like the slump would end at the start of the Salt Lake City Olympics in 2002 either. But with Wayne Gretzky running the team and captain Mario Lemieux leading the way on the ice, Team Canada came on strong. In the final game, they beat Team USA 5–2 to finally end the gold medal drought.

Women's hockey was first introduced to the Olympics at Nagano in 1998, and since Canada had won every Women's World Championship up to that time, they seemed a good bet to win Olympic gold too. Instead, the United States beat Canada in the final game that year. The Americans seemed poised to win again four years later in Salt Lake City, but Hayley Wickenheiser predicted that Canada would win this time and she led her team to a thrilling 3–2 victory over the United States in the gold medal game.

THE GOLDEN GOAL

No Canadian athlete won a gold medal when the Summer Olympics were held in Montreal in 1976. There were no Canadian golds at the Winter Olympics

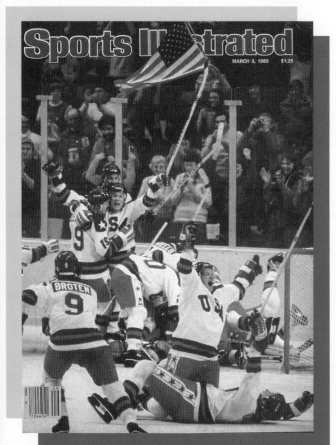

The Miracle on Ice was such an iconic moment in American hockey that *Sports Illustrated* ran this cover showing the winning goal, with no headline at all.

in Calgary in 1988 either. So when Vancouver hosted the Games in 2010, Canadians were promised their athletes would "Own the Podium." But would they? Yes! Canada set a new record for gold medals won. Still, winning the goal medal in men's hockey wasn't going to be easy.

In 2006, NHL rookie Sidney Crosby was left off Canada's Olympic hockey team. But for the Vancouver Games, there was no doubt that he would be there. However, he didn't play as well as people had expected. The team wasn't living up to expectations either. They ended the opening round with a 5–3 loss to the United States before finally springing to life. Canada scored an easy 8–2 win over Germany, and then beat Russia 7–3 in the quarter-finals. Canada seemed to have its semifinal with Slovakia well in hand, but then two late goals turned a 3–0 lead into a 3–2 nail-biter. It took a great save from Roberto Luongo in the final seconds to preserve the victory.

Facing the United States again in the gold medal game, Canada was leading 2–1 with time running out. Then American Zach Parise beat Luongo with just 25 seconds to go. The game headed into overtime. At 7:40 of the extra period, Crosby took a short pass from Jarome Iginla and snuck a quick shot past American goalie Ryan Miller. Team Canada had a 3–2 victory.

THE GREATEST GAME: WOMEN'S EDITION

The gold medal game at the 2014 Winter Olympics may have been the most exciting game in the history of women's hockey! At least if you're a Canadian. For Americans, it was a heartbreaking loss.

For 56 minutes and 34 seconds, Team USA seemed to have the win well in hand. They were leading Team Canada 2–0 and their goalie, Jessie Vetter, looked unbeatable. Then, with 3:26 remaining, Brianne Jenner finally got Canada on the scoreboard. The Canadians pulled their goalie, and the Americans just missed clinching the game when a long, slow shot bounced off Canada's goalpost. Canada was still alive!

With just 55 seconds to go, Canada's Marie-Philip Poulin snapped in a shot for the tying goal. It would take overtime to decide the winner, and when Poulin scored again at 8:10 of the extra period, it gave Team Canada a thrilling 3–2 victory — and their fourth straight Olympic gold medal.

JUNIOR JUBILATION

There have been many memorable moments for Canadian fans at the World Junior Hockey Championship. Two of the best involved two tense semifinals. In a thrilling game against Russia in 2009, Jordan Eberle tied the score with just 5.4 seconds left in the third period, and then got the game-winner in a shootout to give Canada a 6–5 victory. Two years earlier, in 2007, Jonathan Toews scored three goals during an extended shootout to help Canada beat the United States. In both of those years, Canada went on to win the gold medal, but those semifinal games are what fans remember the most.

Team Canada's Marie-Philip Poulin scores the tying goal in the Olympic gold medal game at the Bolshoy Ice Dome in Sochi, Russia, which took place on February 20, 2014.

CAREERS IN HOCKEY

Maybe you're not the best player on your team. That doesn't really matter, as long as you're having fun. Besides, even the best players will have a tough time making it all the way to the NHL. There are many more careers in the hockey world than just the ones on the ice. If you're a talented writer, you could be a hockey reporter for a newspaper or a website. You might even write a book about hockey. If you want to be a doctor, dentist or chiropractor, you may be able to work for a hockey team. There are also lawyers and accountants on staff. And even if all you ever wanted to do was drive the Zamboni machine, there could be a job for you someday with an NHL team. Here are just some positions to consider:

Arena Maintenance
Equipment Manager
Marketing Director
Memorabilia/Merchandise
Photographer
Referee
Scoreboard Operator
Video Coordinator

Saturday Night Is Hockey Night

For someone who never played in the NHL, Ron MacLean is one of the biggest names in hockey. He's hosted CBC coverage of the Olympics and plenty of other sports, too, but fans know him best for his work on *Hockey Night in Canada* and with Don Cherry on *Coach's Corner*.

Ron played football in high school in Red Deer, Alberta, and thought about becoming a teacher. But when he was 16, he got a part-time job at a local radio station. By 18, he was working full-time as a disc jockey. Later, he became a TV weatherman and began working on Red Deer Rustlers junior hockey broadcasts. In 1984, Ron was hired to host Calgary Flames telecasts. In 1986, he moved to Toronto to work on Maple Leafs games and fill in occasionally on *Hockey Night in Canada*. On March 21, 1987, Ron took over as the permanent host of *Hockey Night in Canada*. With just a short gap in between, he's been doing the job ever since. He's also been the host of *Rogers Hometown Hockey* since those Sunday night broadcasts began in 2014.

Watching hockey is a big part of Ron's job. During the week, he

Ron MacLean and Don Cherry on the set of Hockey Night in Canada.

watches hockey almost every night. "I sit with a notepad from 7 p.m. to 1 a.m. and make notes about key plays," he says. "Don Cherry does the same thing." On Fridays, Ron emails his notes to the CBC so they can have highlights ready for *Coach's Corner*. Saturday morning at 9:30, he calls Don Cherry and they discuss topics for the show.

Ron arrives at the CBC studio around 1:30 in the afternoon on Saturdays and prepares to go on the air at 6:30. He writes out ideas for what he wants to say, but likes to ad lib a lot of his conversations. Ron does most of his broadcasting before the game and during intermissions. When the game is on, he watches from a room with six TVs so that he can keep up with that night's action all over the NHL.

Early Days

There was no such thing as TV or radio in the early days of hockey. Newspapers provided the only coverage. But when teams were involved in big games out of town, their fans didn't want to wait until the next day's newspaper came out to read all about it. Newspapers relied on telegraph lines — an early method of long-distance communication — to send them reports on road games. As early as the 1890s, people began gathering in public places to hear someone read snippets of those telegraphed reports. On March 21, 1922, a radio station in Vancouver had an announcer read reports telegraphed from a Stanley Cup game in Toronto on the air for local fans. Though it wasn't truly live play-by-play, this may well have been the first time a hockey game was broadcast on the radio.

Live on the Air

Many believe that Hockey Hall of Fame broadcaster Foster Hewitt called the first live hockey game on Toronto radio station CFCA on March 22, 1923. However, Norman Albert called the first game on February 8, 1923. Foster Hewitt actually broadcast his first game eight days later, on February 16.

Hockey Night in Canada

Foster Hewitt made his first national broadcast of a Toronto Maple Leafs game across a Canada-wide radio network in 1929. In 1931, he called the first game played at Maple Leaf Gardens. In 1936, Hewitt's Saturday night radio broadcasts moved to the CBC and became known as *Hockey Night in Canada*. The move to television came in 1952. The first game on TV was a French broadcast from Montreal, on October 11, 1952, with announcer René Lecavalier. Foster Hewitt made the first English TV broadcast of *Hockey Night in Canada from Toronto* on November 1, 1952.

Legendary broadcaster Foster Hewitt coined the famous phrase "He shoots, he scores!"

Legendary Voices

Since 1984, the Hockey Hall of Fame has honoured great broadcasters with the Foster Hewitt Memorial Award. Hewitt was born in Toronto on November 21, 1902. His father, William A. Hewitt, was sports editor of the *Toronto Star* and secretary of the Ontario Hockey Association, so Foster grew up around sports. When the *Star* set up radio station CFCA in 1922, Foster got a job as a staff announcer. He called all sorts of sporting events over the next few years and became the radio voice of the Toronto Maple Leafs in 1927. After his broadcasts went national, his excited cry, "He shoots, he scores!" soon made him even more famous than the hockey players he was talking about.

Famous as Foster Hewitt was, many older hockey fans believe there has never been a better play-by-play broadcaster than Danny Gallivan. Gallivan was born in Sydney, Nova Scotia, on April 11, 1917. He began his radio career in nearby Antigonish and later became the sports director of a station in Halifax. In 1952, Gallivan became the English radio voice of the Montreal Canadiens. A year later, he began calling games from Montreal for *Hockey Night in Canada* on television.

What made Danny Gallivan such a memorable broadcaster were the colourful descriptions he came up with. Hard shots were "cannonading drives" and great saves were "scintillating." Gallivan made up the word "spinarama" to describe the way a player would whirl to avoid a check. Today, "spinarama" has its own entry in the *Canadian Oxford Dictionary*.

Living Legend Willie O'Ree

Willie O'Ree became the first black player in NHL history when he played two games with the Boston Bruins on January 18, 1958, against the Montreal Canadiens. He played just one more game that season, but returned to play another 43 games with the Bruins during the 1960–61 season.

O'Ree's NHL career may have been brief, but he had a very long career in professional hockey, from 1955 to 1979. From 1961–62 to 1973–74, O'Ree was one of the best — and most popular — players in the Western Hockey League, a top minor league. What made it even more remarkable is that he had lost almost all of the vision in his right eye.

Long after his playing career ended, Willie O'Ree was named the first Director of Youth Development for the NHL/USA Hockey Diversity Task Force in 1998.

Hockey Night in Punjabi

In an effort to attract new Canadians and people who don't normally watch the sport, *Hockey Night in Canada* began broadcasting in different languages in 2007. Over the next few years, there were broadcasts in Italian, Inuktitut, Hindu, Mandarin Chinese, Cantonese and Punjabi. The Punjabi broadcasts have outlasted them all. Harnarayan Singh has done the play-by-play since *Hockey Night in Canada Punjabi* began in 2008.

Singh's parents immigrated from India to Brooks, Alberta, in 1966. He was born in 1984 and says that hockey helped him to feel Canadian while he was growing up. Singh studied broadcasting at university and later worked at TSN and a CBC radio station in Calgary. In addition to his play-by-play work in Punjabi, Singh made history on November 30, 2016, when he became the first Sikh to work an English-language hockey broadcast in

Willie O'Ree was born on October 15, 1935, in Fredericton, New Brunswick. On April 7, 2010, he received the Order of Canada, honoured as a hockey pioneer and dedicated youth mentor.

Bhola Chauhan, left, does the analysis and Harnarayan Singh does the play-by-play for *Hockey Night in Canada Punjabi.* Singh's colourful calls are often shared on social media.

Canada. He served as a rinkside reporter that night for a game between Toronto and Calgary.

Coordinating the Media

TV, radio, newspapers, magazines, websites. All of these media outlets — especially in Canada! — have reporters who want to cover hockey games. Who arranges for them to get seats in the press box? Who makes sure they have access to players for interviews? Who prepares the game notes and statistics they need?

Every team in the NHL has a communications department with three or four men and women who help to coordinate information and deal with requests from the media. Many of the men and women who work in these jobs have degrees or diplomas in communications or sports management. There are lots of perks to a job like this, such as watching the games live and getting to know the players, but it's not all fun. The hours can be very long, and things have to get done fast. That's especially true on game days when the media wants stories beginning with a team's morning skate and needs more ending late at night when the game is over.

Social Media

These days, teams do a lot of their own reporting, too. They all have websites and Twitter accounts and they need people to run those and get their stories out. Sometimes, these jobs are done by the communications department, but these days most teams have a separate social media department or a social media coordinator. So, if you like hockey and you're good with your smart phone, there could be a job for you some day tweeting for your favourite NHL team.

Power Skaters

Many of the off-ice jobs in the NHL are handled by men and women, but on the ice, it's always been men. Who knows if we'll ever see a female player in the NHL, but just before the 2016–17 season, the NHL got its first full-time female coach. Dawn Braid was hired by the Arizona Coyotes as the team's skating coach.

While the job in Arizona was Braid's first full-time NHL position, she already had a long association with the league. She'd worked part-time for the Coyotes and also served as a skating consultant with the Toronto Maple Leafs, Anaheim Ducks, Buffalo Sabres and Calgary Flames. In addition, Braid spent seven years with the Athlete Training Centre in Mississauga, Ontario, as director of skating development. Among the skaters she worked with there are NHL stars John Tavares, Jason Spezza and Mike Cammalleri.

Braid is a former figure skater who first started coaching hockey players back in 1984. Former world champion pairs figure skater Barb Underhill has been working as a skating consultant with the Toronto Maple Leafs since 2012.

Fixing Their Aches and Pains

Hockey is a fast-paced, tiring and very physical game. Who do hockey players turn to when they have aches and pains? Unless an injury is so bad that it has to be treated by the doctors, dentists, surgeons and other specialists all teams have on staff, the first line of defence is the athletic therapist.

On days when a team is practising, the athletic therapist and his assistants have

Dawn Braid is the skating coach for the Arizona Coyotes.

to be there very early to begin treating players with injuries from previous games. Once practice starts, they have to be nearby in case anyone gets hurt on the ice. Then, when practice is over, there's more treatment for any lingering ailments before the players can leave the rink. On game days, there's a similar routine before and after the team's morning skate. When the players return for the game, the therapists get them started on their stretching and exercise routines. They've always got to be around during the game in case of injuries, and often have to stay late afterward to help players with any other problems they may have.

Like many jobs in hockey, being an athletic therapist means putting in long hours. It also takes a long time just to learn how to do the job. Not only do therapists need a university degree (usually in health and physical education, or a similar field), they need to do another specialized three-year program in order to get the certification needed to work in the NHL.

By the Numbers

Do you like numbers? Are you good at math? Do you enjoy solving puzzles? Are you good with a computer? If so, you could have a career in the NHL as a statistician or in statistical analysis.

In the early days of the NHL, statisticians worked with pencils and pads of paper, which they used to record who got each goal, assist and penalty. Sometimes they would record shots on goal, too. As the years went by, the statisticians also noted all of the players who were on the ice when each goal was scored.

It wasn't until the 1980s that the NHL started using computers to record its statistics. As computers improved, more and more statistics could be tracked. By 2008, the NHL was noting every shot and blocked shot, every faceoff, every hit, every time a player gave away the puck and every second that each player was on the ice.

In recent years, people have been using computers and video recordings of games to come up with brand new statistics. These new stats are often referred to as analytics. They are designed to better understand how and why things happen on the ice, and which players are making hidden contributions beyond the standard player statistics. Analyzing this new data is the key. Teams can now track such things as where the puck was shot from when a goal went in, and try to develop strategies from that.

When people talk about hockey analytics, they often refer to Corsi and Fenwick. Corsi is named after former Buffalo Sabres goalie coach Jim Corsi. This stat measures all the shot attempts taken by a team, even if those shots are blocked or miss the net. Fenwick is named after Calgary Flames fan and engineer Matt Fenwick, who wrote a popular hockey blog. It's similar to Corsi, but it doesn't count blocked shots. The NHL calls these two stats Shot Attempts (SAT) and Unblocked Shot Attempts (USAT). When a team or a player has higher numbers in these statistics, it indicates that they have the puck more often. Teams that have the puck more often tend to score more goals, and teams that score more goals tend to win more hockey games.

STANDARD PLAYER STATISTICS

GP: Games Played

G: Goals

A: Assists

Pts: Points

PIM: Penalties in Minutes

PP: Power-Play Goals (sometimes PPG)

    Goals scored while the other team has a player serving a penalty.

SH: Shorthanded Goals (sometimes SHG)

    Goals scored while the scoring team has a player serving a penalty.

GW: Game-Winning Goals (Sometimes GWG)

S: Shots

%: Shooting Percentage

    Calculated by dividing the number of goals a player has scored by the number of shots he has taken and multiplying by 100. For example, for a player with 43 goals on 249 shots, his shooting percentage would be 43 / 249 x 100 = 17.3

+/-: Plus-Minus

    The difference between goals scored by a player's team and the goals scored against it while the player is on the ice. Only even-strength goals and shorthanded goals count.

TF: Total Faceoffs

    The number of times this player has taken a faceoff.

F%: Faceoff Winning Percentage

    Calculated by dividing the number of faceoffs a player has won by the number of faceoffs he has taken and multiplied by 100. For example, for a player who has won 675 face-offs out 1,137 total face-offs his face-off winning percentage would be 675 / 1137 x 100 = 59.4.

TOI: Time On Ice Per Game (sometimes abbreviated as TOI/G or Min for minutes)

STANDARD GOALIE STATISTICS

GS: Games Started

W: Wins

L: Loses

O/T: Overtime Losses/ties

Min: Minutes Played (sometimes abbreviated as TOI for Time On Ice)

GA: Goals Against

SO: Shutouts

GAA: Goals-Against Average (sometimes abbreviated as Avg)

    Calculated by dividing a goalie's total number of goals against by his minutes played and multiplying by 60. For example, for a goalie with 152 goals against in 4,007 minutes played, his goals-against average would be 152 / 4007 x 60 = 2.28.

SA: Shots Against

SV: Saves

S%: Save Percentage

    Calculated by dividing a goalie's saves by his shots against. For example, for a goalie who makes 1878 saves on 2040 shots against, his save percentage would be 1878 / 2040 = .921.

A HALL OF FAME CAREER

You may already know some things about Phil Pritchard. If you do, it's probably because he's one of the "Keepers of the Stanley Cup." Phil is one of a few people who get to travel with the Stanley Cup whenever it goes on display somewhere. He and his colleague Craig Campbell, wearing their trademark blazers and white gloves, are the ones who carry the Stanley Cup out onto the ice for presentation each year when a team wins it. But there's a lot more to what Phil does than accompanying the Stanley Cup. Phil is the vice president and curator at the Hockey Hall of Fame, where he has worked since 1988.

"I knew I wanted to do something in hockey," Phil says. So he went to Durham College in Oshawa, Ontario, to study sports administration. Since getting the job at the Hockey Hall of Fame, he has also taken courses relating to library, resource centre and archival management. "I love coming to work in the morning," Phil says. "It's always a good day when you're involved in hockey."

A typical day for Phil can involve anything from research to public relations, travelling with the NHL trophies or setting up displays of hockey memorabilia. All the time away from his family can be hard, but Phil understands that hockey is a form of entertainment, and entertainers have to spend a lot of time on the road.

"Keeper of the Cup" Phil Pritchard with Craig Campbell of the Hockey Hall of Fame

THE TROPHY ROOM

YOU'VE GOTTA HAVE HART

Awarded each year to the league's most valuable player, the Hart Trophy is the greatest individual honour in the NHL. It is also the league's oldest trophy. It was donated to the NHL at a special league meeting on February 9, 1924, and presented for the first time at the end of the 1923–24 season. The first winner was Frank Nighbor, a future Hockey Hall of Famer who was then starring with the original Ottawa Senators.

Rob Riggle, host of the 2015 NHL awards, onstage with trophies. Top (left to right) Bill Masterton Trophy, General Manager of the Year Award, William M. Jennings Trophy, James Norris Trophy. Bottom (left to right) Ted Lindsay Award, Hart Trophy, Art Ross Trophy, Vezina Trophy.

The Hart Trophy was donated to the NHL by Dr. David Hart of Montreal. His son, Cecil Hart, was a sports executive in the city and a future coach of the Montreal Canadiens. The original Hart Trophy was a tall, skinny cup. In February of 1960, NHL owners voted to retire the old trophy. They replaced it with a new one, which is still in use today. The new trophy — officially dubbed the Hart Memorial Trophy — was designed to look like a flaming torch.

The winner of the Hart Trophy is selected in a vote by members of the Professional Hockey Writers' Association in every NHL city immediately after the regular season.

THE PLAYERS' MVP

In 1971, the NHL Players' Association (NHLPA) created its own MVP trophy. It was named after former Canadian Prime Minister Lester B. Pearson. In 2010, the trophy was renamed the Ted Lindsay Award. Lindsay was an NHL star in the 1950s and 1960s who helped form the NHL players' union. NHL players vote on this award.

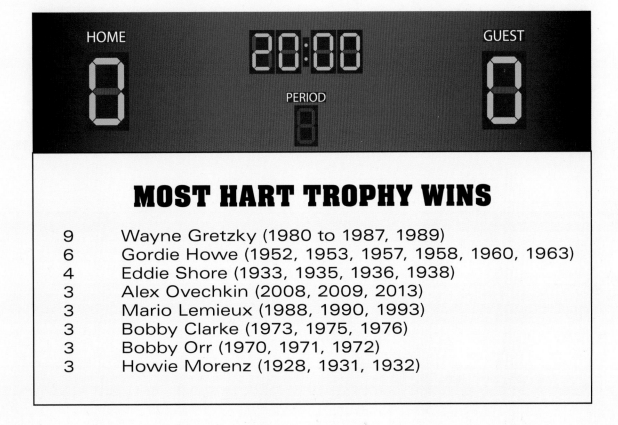

MOST HART TROPHY WINS

9	Wayne Gretzky (1980 to 1987, 1989)
6	Gordie Howe (1952, 1953, 1957, 1958, 1960, 1963)
4	Eddie Shore (1933, 1935, 1936, 1938)
3	Alex Ovechkin (2008, 2009, 2013)
3	Mario Lemieux (1988, 1990, 1993)
3	Bobby Clarke (1973, 1975, 1976)
3	Bobby Orr (1970, 1971, 1972)
3	Howie Morenz (1928, 1931, 1932)

A SPORTING LADY

Lord Julian Byng was governor general of Canada from 1921 to 1926. He and his wife, Lady Evelyn Byng, were from England, but they both fell in love with hockey while living in Ottawa. In 1925, Lady Byng donated a trophy to the NHL. It is awarded "to the player adjudged to have exhibited the best type of sportsmanship and gentlemanly conduct combined with a high standard of playing ability." The first winner in 1924–25 was Frank Nighbor.

When Frank Boucher of the New York Rangers won the Lady Byng Trophy seven times in eight seasons from 1927–28 through 1934–35, he was given the original trophy to keep. Lady Byng donated a new trophy in 1936. After her death in 1949, the NHL donated another new trophy and called it the Lady Byng Memorial Trophy.

The winner of the Lady Byng Trophy is selected in a vote by members of the Professional Hockey Writers' Association immediately after the regular season.

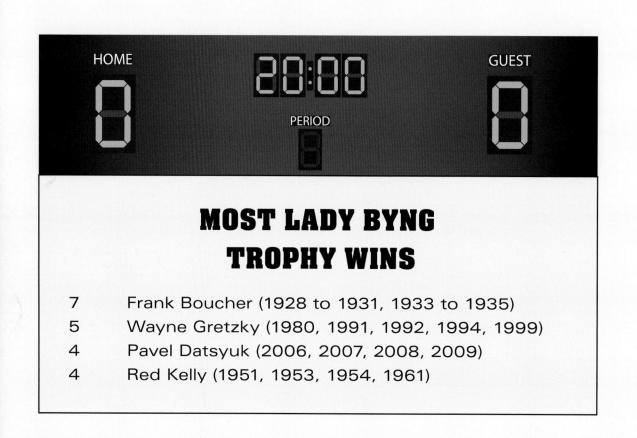

HOME 8 20:00 GUEST 8

PERIOD

MOST LADY BYNG TROPHY WINS

7   Frank Boucher (1928 to 1931, 1933 to 1935)
5   Wayne Gretzky (1980, 1991, 1992, 1994, 1999)
4   Pavel Datsyuk (2006, 2007, 2008, 2009)
4   Red Kelly (1951, 1953, 1954, 1961)

MOST VEZINA TROPHY WINS

7	Jacques Plante* (1956 to 1960, 1962, 1969[†])
6	Dominik Hasek (1994, 1995, 1997 to 1999, 2001)
6	Bill Durnan* (1944 to 1947, 1949, 1950)
5	Ken Dryden* (1973, 1976, 1977 to 1979[∫])
4	Martin Brodeur (2003, 2004, 2007, 2008)
4	Michel Laroque* (1977 to 1979[∫], 1981**)
4	Terry Sawchuk* (1952, 1953, 1955, 1965[‡])
4	Tiny Thompson* (1930, 1933, 1936, 1938)

* all wins for allowing fewest goals against
† shared with St. Louis teammate Glenn Hall
∫ shared by Montreal teammates Ken Dryden and Michel Larocque
** shared with Montreal teammates Richard Sevigny and Wayne Thomas
‡ shared with Toronto teammate Johnny Bower in 1964–65

THE MEN IN THE NETS

The trophy awarded to the best goalie in the NHL each year is named in honour of Georges Vezina. Vezina joined the Montreal Canadiens in 1910–11 when the team played in the National Hockey Association. He played every game in goal for the Canadiens from that season until the end of the 1924–25 NHL campaign.

Including regular season and playoffs, that was 367 games in a row. He also helped the Canadiens win the Stanley Cup in 1916 and 1924 and posted the best average in the NHL during the league's first season of 1917–18.

Vezina's streak of games ended on November 28, 1925, when chest pains forced him out of action. He never played again and died of tuberculosis on March 26, 1926. At the end of the 1926–27 season the Montreal Canadiens donated the Vezina Trophy in his memory. The first winner that year was the Canadiens' new goalie, George Hainsworth. In fact, Hainsworth won the trophy three years in a row.

Before the 1981–82 season, the Vezina Trophy was awarded to the goalie (or goalies) on the NHL team that allowed the fewest goals against. Since then, the trophy has gone to the goalie that is judged to be the best at his position. Voting is conducted by the general managers of every NHL team immediately after the regular season.

REWARDING THE ROOKIES

The trophy that goes to the best first-year player in the NHL is named after the league's first president (now called the commissioner), Frank Calder, who became the first president of the NHL in 1917. He held the job until he died on February 4, 1943.

NHL Award winners from 1972 (left to right): the Chicago Blackhawks' Tony Esposito with the Vezina Trophy; the New York Rangers' Jean Ratelle with the Lady Byng Trophy; the Boston Bruins' Bobby Orr with both the Hart and James Norris awards; and the Montreal Canadiens' Ken Dryden with the Calder Trophy.

Though sportswriters first selected a rookie of the year after the 1932–33 season (the first winner was Carl Voss), there was no official trophy. However, in 1936–37 Calder presented the first trophy and had a new one minted every year. After his death, the NHL presented a permanent trophy, officially known as the Calder Memorial Trophy.

The winner of the Calder is selected in a vote by members of the Professional Hockey Writers' Association immediately after the regular season.

THE ART OF SCORING

The Art Ross Trophy goes to the top scorer in the NHL, but Art Ross only scored one goal in his short three-game NHL career. However, he had been one of the best defencemen in hockey before the NHL was formed.

Ross joined the Boston Bruins as coach and general manager in 1924. He remained with the Bruins, in various front office roles, until 1954. Ross first planned to donate a trophy to the NHL in 1941. Ross's trophy was supposed to go to the most valuable player in the league. However, the NHL already had the Hart Trophy for that. Ross wanted the players to vote for his trophy instead of the sportswriters. But this trophy was never presented.

Finally, in June of 1948, the NHL accepted a new trophy donated by Art Ross and his sons, Art Jr. and John, which would go to the leading scorer.

Elmer Lach of the Montreal Canadiens was the trophy's first winner in the 1947–48 season.

A CASE FOR THE DEFENCE

James Norris was a wealthy grain merchant from Montreal who had moved to Chicago. When the NHL added a team there in 1926, Norris hoped to buy it. He didn't get a chance, but in 1932, Norris bought the NHL team in Detroit. Knowing Detroit's car-building reputation as "the Motor City," Norris borrowed the winged-wheel logo of the Montreal Amateur Athletic Association for his team's sweaters. He also changed the team name from Detroit Falcons to Detroit Red Wings.

James Norris passed away on December 4, 1952. His family would continue to own the team until 1982, but the children wanted to do something to honour their father. The family donated the James Norris Memorial Trophy to the NHL on September 24, 1953, to reward the NHL's best defenceman. The reason may have been that Norris himself had played defence as a boy in Montreal, or just that he had always appreciated tough defensive play. The first winner of the Norris Trophy at the end of the 1953–54 season was Detroit's Red Kelly.

Each year, the winner of the Norris Trophy is selected in a vote by members of the Professional Hockey Writers' Association immediately after the regular season.

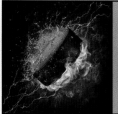

The Other Goalie Trophy

Since the 1981–82 season, the goalie (or goalies) on the team that allows the fewest goals-against has been awarded the William Jennings Trophy. In order to qualify, a goalie must have played at least 25 games for his team. William Jennings was a long-time member of the New York Rangers front office and one of the great builders of hockey in the United States . . . but he was never a goalie.

MVPP: MOST VALUABLE PLAYOFF PLAYER

Every year since 1965, the most valuable player in the playoffs has been presented with the Conn Smythe Trophy. The trophy was donated by the Toronto Maple Leafs in honour of the team's long-time owner, Conn Smythe. The trophy was designed as a small silver model of Maple Leaf Gardens (home to the Maple Leafs until 1999), which Smythe had built in 1931. The first winner of the Conn Smythe Trophy, in 1965, was Montreal Canadiens captain Jean Beliveau. Goalie Patrick Roy has won it the most. Roy won with Montreal in 1986 and 1993 and with the Colorado Avalanche in 2001. In the early years of the trophy, the governors of the NHL teams voted on the winner. Since 1971, sportswriters have voted for the Conn Smythe Trophy winner immediately after the final game of the playoffs.

A MEMORIAL TO MASTERTON

Bill Masterton was born in Winnipeg, Manitoba, on August 13, 1938. When he was 19, Masterton left Manitoba to play hockey at the University of Denver.

Masterton hoped to be one of the few players who made it to the NHL from American colleges. After four years at the school and two U.S. university championships, Masterton graduated in 1961. The league had only six teams, and Masterton had to spend several years in the minors. Finally, when the NHL doubled in size for the 1967–68 season, Masterton got his chance.

Almost no players in the NHL wore helmets in those days. In a game on January 13, 1968, Masterton tumbled awkwardly after a check and hit his head on the ice. He was knocked unconscious and suffered a serious brain injury. Masterton died two days later. He is the only player in NHL history to die from an injury sustained in a game.

There was a lot of talk about helmets after Masterton's death, but it took until 1979 before the NHL passed a rule making them mandatory. The league was much quicker to name a trophy in Masterton's honour. Officially known as the William Masterton Memorial Trophy, the award was donated by the Professional Hockey Writers' Association and accepted by the NHL on February 20, 1968. The award goes to a player who exhibits perseverance, sportsmanship and dedication to hockey. The first winner, after the

MOST ART ROSS TROPHY WINS

10	Wayne Gretzky (1981 to 1987, 1990, 1991, 1994)
6	Mario Lemieux (1988, 1989, 1992, 1993, 1996, 1997)
6	Gordie Howe (1951 to 1954, 1957, 1963)
5	Jaromir Jagr (1995, 1998 to 2001)
5	Phil Esposito (1969, 1971 to 1974)
4	Stan Mikita (1964, 1965, 1967, 1968)

1967–68 season, was Claude Provost of the Montreal Canadiens.

Every winter, hockey writers in each NHL city vote for a local nominee for the Masterton Trophy. At the end of the season, the writers vote again to determine a winner from among the players nominated.

TEAM TROPHIES

In addition to the Stanley Cup, there are three other team trophies. The team that finishes with the best record in the overall standings at the end of the regular season receives the Presidents' Trophy. This award was presented to the NHL by the league's Board of Governors and was first handed out after the 1985–86 season.

Prince Edward of England (the future King Edward VIII, and the uncle of Queen Elizabeth) donated the Prince of Wales Trophy to the NHL in 1925. Over the years, it has been awarded

IN THE CREASE

Though NHL rookie Wayne Gretzky tied for the league lead with 137 points during the 1979–1980 season, he was ineligible to win the Calder. The rules at that time stated that a player could not have played for a professional league before joining the NHL; Gretzky had played a full season with the WHA as a 17-year-old the year before.

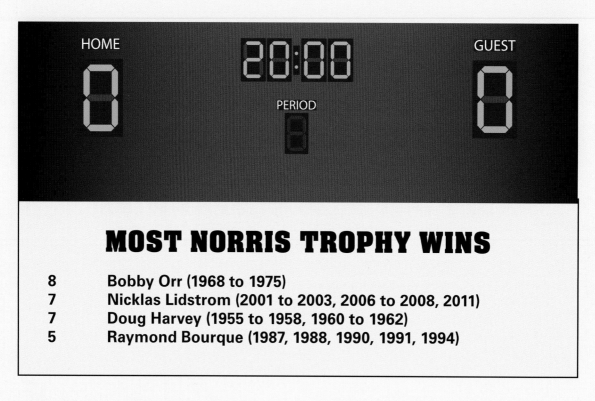

HOME

20:00

GUEST

PERIOD

MOST NORRIS TROPHY WINS

8 **Bobby Orr (1968 to 1975)**
7 **Nicklas Lidstrom (2001 to 2003, 2006 to 2008, 2011)**
7 **Doug Harvey (1955 to 1958, 1960 to 1962)**
5 **Raymond Bourque (1987, 1988, 1990, 1991, 1994)**

for a number of different things, but since the 1993–94 season it has gone to the playoff champion of the Eastern Conference.

The Clarence Campbell Bowl goes to the winner of the Western Conference. It was donated to the NHL in 1968 in honour of long-time NHL president Clarence Campbell. Like the Prince of Wales Trophy, the Campbell Bowl has also been awarded for several different things over the years. If you're watching TV when either of these trophies is presented after the Conference Finals, you'll often see that players won't pick them up. That's because of a superstition that picking up these trophies will jinx you against winning the Stanley Cup.

Can They Keep Them?

When a player is announced as a winner at the NHL Awards show, he doesn't get to keep the award or trophy, though sometimes the winners get to appear with it at public events. Since the 1980s, winners have received mini trophies to keep.

P. K. Subban poses with the miniature James Norris Memorial Trophy he gets to keep after he was named winner for the 2012–13 NHL season. The large trophy on the right is the Vezina Trophy.

OTHER MAJOR AWARDS

Jack Adams Award
Awarded to: Coach of the year
Named for: Long-time Detroit Red Wings coach and general manager

Frank J. Selke Trophy
Awarded to: Best defensive forward
Named for: Long-time Montreal Canadiens general manager

King Clancy Memorial Trophy
Awarded for: Leadership qualities and contributions to charity
Named for: Long-time NHL player, coach, referee and executive

Maurice "Rocket" Richard Trophy
Awarded to: Leading goal scorer
Named for: Montreal Canadiens legendary scorer

HOCKEY TALK

Attacking zone: The part of the ice inside the opponent's blue line.

Backchecking: Offensive players coming back into their own end to help the defencemen handle the other team.

Backhand: A shot taken, or pass made, with the back part of the blade of the stick.

Blade: The bottom part of a stick, used for shooting or passing the puck. Also, the steel runner on the bottom of a skate.

Between the pipes: A term for playing goal (because the goalie net has two metal posts at each side).

Boards: The wall that surrounds the ice surface. NHL rules say the boards must be at least 40 inches (101 cm) high, but not more than 48 inches (122 cm).

Breakaway: When the puck carrier moves in alone on the goalie, with no teammates or opposing players in between them.

Butterfly: A style where the goalie drops to his knees to cover the lower part of the net.

Captain: The leader of the team and the only player who is supposed to be allowed to question the referee on the ice. The captain wears a C on his sweater. Players known as assistant captains, or alternate captains, wear an A on their sweaters.

Center: A forward who usually plays in the middle part of the ice and is often responsible for taking faceoffs.

Changing on the fly: Switching players while the play is still going on instead of waiting for a faceoff.

Check: To hit another player with your body, usually the shoulder, to bump them off the puck.

Checker/Checking line: A player whose best skill is to prevent the other team's best players from scoring. A forward line whose primary responsibility is to play defensively.

Cherry picking: When a player hangs around the other team's zone waiting for a pass.

Clear the puck: Shooting the puck out of the defensive zone.

Clutch-and-grab: A defensive style used to slow down the other team.

Coast-to-coast: When a player carries the puck from deep inside his own zone all the way to the other end of the ice.

Colour commentator: An announcer on TV or radio who gives his analysis of the play.

Crashing the net: A player or players heading straight for the goalie or the front of the other team's net at high speed.

Crease: The area of the ice directly in front of the net that is painted blue. There is not supposed to be any contact with the goalie when he is in his crease.

Dangle: Moving with the puck, dipping and darting, to keep it away from other players and get a chance for a shot on goal.

Deke: Similar to dangle, but usually just a few quick moves to get around a player or a goalie.

Defensive zone: The part of the ice inside a team's own blue line.

Delayed penalty: When a player on one team gets a penalty, but the other team still has possession of the puck. The referee does not blow his whistle until the team that got the penalty gets the puck.

Drop pass: A pass made from a player to a teammate who is behind him.

Dump and chase: A strategy of shooting the puck into the other team's zone and then skating hard after it.

Empty-net goal: When a team scores a goal after the other team's goalie has been pulled (removed) from the play for an extra attacker.

Extra attacker: An additional skater who comes on the ice when a team has pulled (removed) its goalie.

Faceoff: The method used to begin play at the beginning of a period or after a stoppage of play.

Five-on-five: When neither team has a penalty, and both teams have all five of their skaters on the ice. (Five-on-four or five-on-three refer to one team having all of its skaters while the other team has a player or two in the penalty box.)

Five hole: The gap between a goalie's legs.

Forechecking: When the attacking team checks the defending team hard in its own zone to try to create scoring chances.

Forward: A forward is any player who plays left wing, right wing or center.

Free agent: When a player does not have a contract with a team and is allowed to sign with any team. In the NHL, unrestricted free agents are free to sign with any other team. Restricted free agents can negotiate with other teams, but their old team is still given the chance to match any new contract.

Freezing the puck: When a player pins the puck against the boards, or a goalie covers it up.

Full strength: When a team has all five of its skaters on the ice.

Give and go: When a player passes the puck to a teammate, and then quickly gets a return pass.

Goal mouth: The area in front of the net, but not a truly defined area like the goal crease.

Go (or going) upstairs: Shooting the puck high. (Like "Top shelf.") Also, when the referee asks for a play to be reviewed by the NHL office.

Hat trick: When one player scores three goals in a game. Scoring three goals in a row is often referred to as a natural hat trick.

Handcuffed: When a player can't quite get his stick on the puck.

Insurance goal: A goal that widens a team's lead, usually to two or three goals, late in a game.

Killing a penalty: When a team that is a man short because of a penalty prevents the other team from scoring. Often referred to as a penalty kill.

Light the lamp: To score a goal and make the red goal light come on.

Line: A combination of the three forwards (centre, left wing and right wing) who are on the ice together.

Linesmen: Two on-ice officials who work with the referee to call the game. The linesmen are responsible for calling offsides and icings. They can also call some penalties. The linesmen are also the ones who have to break up fights.

Loose puck: When the puck is in open ice and neither team has control of it.

Man advantage: When one team has a penalty and has fewer players on the ice, the other team has a man advantage.

Matching lines: When a coach from one team tries to make sure there are certain players on the ice to play against certain players from the other team.

Netminder: Another word for goalie.

Neutral zone: The area in the middle of the ice between the two blue lines.

Neutral zone trap: A defensive strategy that focuses on making it hard for the other team to carry the puck through the neutral zone.

Odd-man rush: When the team carrying the puck has more players in position than the opposing team.

Offside: When a player proceeds across the blue line into the attacking zone ahead of the puck.

Off wing: When a left-winger is on the right side, or a right-winger is on the left side. Or when a player who shoots left plays right wing, or the other way around.

One-on-one: When a puck carrier skates in by himself, facing only one player from the other team.

One-timer: Shooting the puck directly off of a pass without stopping it first.

Overtime: An extra period of play added at the end of the game if the score is tied. During the regular season, overtime is limited to five minutes before going to a shootout if the game is still tied. In the playoffs, overtime lasts as long as it takes for a team to score.

Paddle: The wide portion of a goalie's stick.

Penalty box: The area where a player has to sit when he has been given a penalty.

Period: A segment of playing time. In the NHL, a game is made up of three periods that are each 20 minutes long.

Pine: A slang term referring to the players' bench. A player who is not seeing much ice time is said to be "riding the pine."

Playing the man: When a player (usually a defenceman) continues to cover a player from the other team and allows the puck to be picked up by a teammate.

Playing the puck: When the goalie leaves his crease to handle the puck.

Point-blank: A shot taken from directly in front of the net.

Poke check: A quick move with the stick to knock the puck away from an opponent.

Power forward: A forward who is big and strong and is just as good at scoring goals as playing a physical game.

Power play: When the other team has a penalty, the team that has the man advantage is said to be on the power play.

Prospect: A young player who shows potential to become a good NHL player.

Pulling the goalie: Removing the goalie to get an extra skater on the ice. This is usually done late in a close game when a team really needs a goal, or when a delayed penalty is going to be called.

Quarterback: A term borrowed from football and usually used to describe an offensive defenceman who is good at handling the puck on a power play.

Quick release: A player who can shoot the puck quickly with little time needed to get ready or aim the puck is said to have a quick release.

Ragging the puck: Skating with the puck to waste time, usually when killing a penalty.

Rebound: When the puck bounces off someone, usually a goalie, after a shot.

Referee: The official on the ice who calls penalties and is responsible for controlling the game. In the NHL, there are two referees on the ice, in addition to two linesmen.

Rush: When a player carries the puck up the ice to put his team on the attack.

Salary cap: The maximum amount that a team can spend on the contracts of its players. There is also a minimum lower limit that a team can't spend less than.

Screening: Blocking a goalie's view of the play.

Screen shot: A shot taken while the goalie is being screened.

Shadow: To cover a player very closely or a player that covers another player closely.

Shaft: The long, straight part of a stick that is held by the player.

Shift: The amount of time that a player, or a forward line, or a defensive pair, is on the ice at one time.

Shootout: A method used to break ties in which each team alternates having one player take a shot at the other team's goalie. Also, a high-scoring game.

Short side: The side of the net or the goalie that is closest to the shooter.

Shorthanded: When a team has a penalty and so has fewer players out on the ice then the other team, they are playing shorthanded.

Shutout: When a team or a goalie doesn't give up any goals in a game.

Slapshot: A powerful shot that requires a big windup with the stick.

Slot: The area on the ice in front of a goalie, outside of the crease and between the two faceoff circles.

Snap shot: A quick shot fired with a fast snap of the wrists.

Sniper: A player who is good at scoring goals.

Standing on his head: When a goalie is playing very well to keep his team in the game by making fantastic saves.

Stay-at-home defenceman: A defenceman who concentrates on defensive play and doesn't skate with the puck very much or join the offensive rush.

Stickhandling: Controlling the puck by shifting it quickly from one side of the stick blade to the other.

Stretch pass: A long pass out of the defensive zone, right through the neutral zone and across the centre ice red line to the other team's blue line.

Sudden death: An overtime period that ends as soon as one of the teams scores a goal.

Tie up your man: To check an opposing player closely.

Tip; *tip-in*: To deflect the puck after it's been shot by another player; to deflect the puck into the net.

Toe-Drag: When a player controls the puck with the "toe" (tip) of his stick blade

Top shelf: The upper part of the net. Shooting the puck into the upper part of the net for a goal is sometimes referred to as "going top shelf." (Like "Going upstairs.")

Turnover: When a player gives up possession of the puck to the other team, often because the player giving up the puck has been forced into some kind of mistake.

Two-way player: A player who is good at scoring or setting up goals, and also plays strong defensive hockey.

Two–hundred foot player: Similar to a two-way player, someone who plays a solid game at either end of the ice.

Winger: A forward whose primary zone of play on the ice is along the sides of the playing area. A right-winger is responsible for the right-hand side of the ice and a left-winger is responsible for the left-hand side.

Wraparound: A play in which the puck carrier starts behind the other team's goal line, or at one side of the net, and swings quickly around to the front of the net to try and stuff the puck past the goalie.

Wrist shot: A type of shot that uses arm muscles (especially in the wrist and forearm) to fire the puck.

Zone: One of three areas on the ice. (See "Attacking zone," "Defensive zone" and "Neutral zone.")

OFFICIAL NHL RINK DIMENSIONS

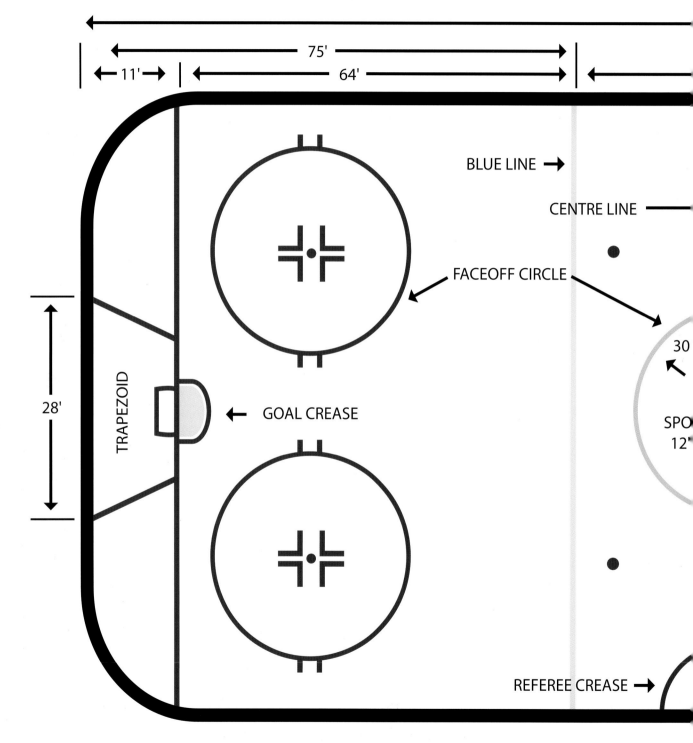

75'

11'

64'

BLUE LINE →

CENTRE LINE

FACEOFF CIRCLE

30

TRAPEZOID

28'

GOAL CREASE ←

SPO
12'

REFEREE CREASE →

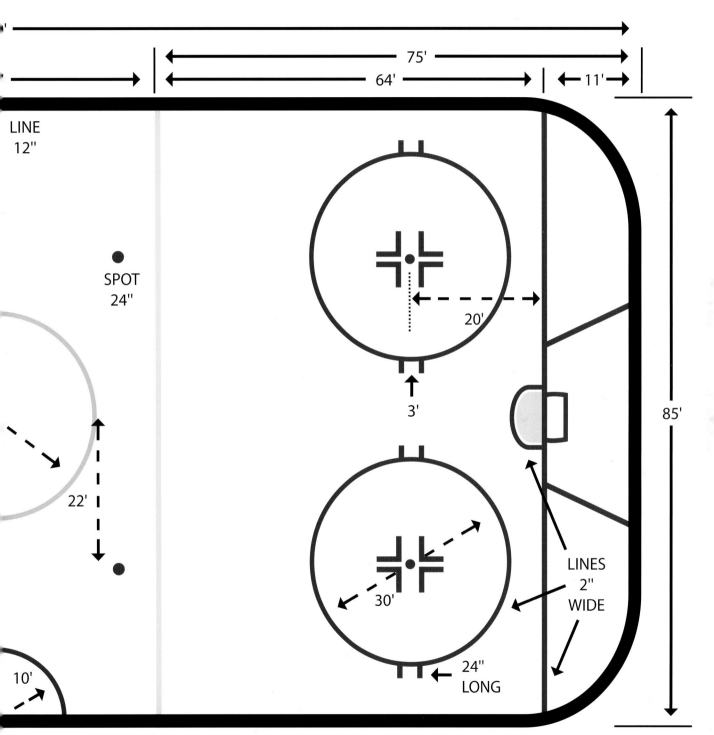

75'

64'

11'

85'

LINE
12"

SPOT
24"

20'

3'

22'

30'

10'

24"
LONG

LINES
2"
WIDE

As in the NHL, international rinks measure 200 feet (61 metres) in length but they are 100 feet (30.5 metres) wide. The distance from the end boards to the goal lines is 13.5 feet (4 metres) but the distance from the end boards to the blue lines is the same 75 feet (22.86 metres). There is no trapezoid area behind the goal lines.

INDEX

FROM THE AUTHOR

THEN AND NOW

I have been writing professionally about sports and sports history since graduating from Trent University in 1985. My first book was published in 1992, and I've been writing books for kids since 1999. I mostly write non-fiction, but I've also written two novels.

As the oldest of three boys in a sports-loving family in Toronto, I learned to ski when I was six, to water ski a few years later, and played hockey, football and baseball while growing up. By the age of 10 I was a budding sports fanatic who was filling his school news assignments with game reports instead of current events. I also helped my father coach my brother's hockey teams, and worked for a couple of years as a referee (which I never really liked). Football was probably my best sport, and I was a pretty good house league hockey player, but I was horrible at baseball. Still, when the Blue Jays were born in 1977, I quickly became a huge fan. My family still has season tickets.

Both my parents were big sports fans. My mother especially loved baseball. She still does. My dad took me to my first NHL hockey game at Maple Leaf Gardens when I was seven years old. But, really, I think what hooked me for life was the famous Summit Series between Canada and Russia in September of 1972. I was only eight, but I'll never forget it. I watched Paul Henderson score the series-winning goal in the last seconds of the final game on a TV in my grade four classroom. Ask your parents — or your grandparents — and if they were living anywhere in Canada in 1972, I'll bet they remember it too!

As a boy, I was the type of student who was always being told he needed to work harder! School just wasn't as much fun as sports. My grade five teacher used to scold me for filling those news assignments with sports stories. I do wish I'd worked a little bit harder in school, but today I make my living writing about sports and looking up stories to share with readers like you. I hope you enjoy them! Not many of us will grow up to play in the NHL, or represent our country at the Olympics. It doesn't mean we can't have fun playing hockey, wherever the game takes us.